CONTENTS

Needed:
Skills for Christian Parents

I'm worried that Pam is getting involved in drugs at school. But whenever I bring it up, she gets mad and just won't talk.

Tim is just unmanageable. He's into everything — dresser drawers, book shelves, even my best china! I put him in his playpen — and he just yowls.

Homework is a perpetual hassle at our house.

Susan dawdles and dawdles until I could just scream!

All through their childhood years our kids went to church with us. Now that they're grown, only Mark attends. I don't know where we went wrong.

These are actual complaints made in parent classes I've led — in a church and in a public school setting. Regardless of the setting, the complaints are quite similar. Kids are "turning off" their parents — and the parents are concerned.

When we talk to the kids — particularly adolescents — much of the same pain of ruptured and strained relationships comes through:

I can never really talk with my parents.

All they ever do is preach.

Sure, I've tried grass. So what? My parents drink. As far as I'm concerned, they're a bunch of phonies.

What Does the Bible Say?

So what else is new? Eve sinned. Adam blamed his wife. And their firstborn son killed his brother.

Photo by John Pearson

Ham ridiculed his drunken father.

Ishmael teased Isaac.

Isaac favored Esau. His wife favored Jacob.

Jacob tricked his brother out of his birthright.

And Jacob's sons sold their brother into slavery.

It looks like a pretty bad record even for the people of God in their family life.

And yet — does it have to be?

The Bible presents a haunting picture of what a family in Christ *could* be:

> Always and for everything giving thanks in the name of our Lord Jesus Christ to God the Father, being subject to one another out of reverence for Christ.
>
> Wives subject to husbands as to the Lord. . . . Husbands loving wives, as Christ loved the church and gave Himself up for her. . . .
>
> Children obeying parents in the Lord. . . .
>
> Fathers not provoking children to anger. . . .
>
> Ephesians 5:21 — 6:4

Needed: Specific Skills for Specific Situations

Sounds great! But how does it work out in action? What specifically do I *do* when —

> I want to go out to dinner and my wife says she's tired?
>
> It's time for Steve to go to bed, and he pleads that he's still got homework to do?
>
> Cheri says, "You're not being fair!"
>
> My daughter's room is a mess (even though she'd agreed to straighten it out), and now she asks whether she may go to a movie.

Take that last situation. Just last Sunday, in a class I lead at church, one parent said:

"I'd tell her, 'First clean up your room. Then you can go.' "

Another said: "The messy room wouldn't bother me. It's *her* room. If it bothers us, we just close the door."

Which angered another parent: "That's the trouble with parents today. We let kids do whatever they please. And they never learn any responsibility. Now when I was young . . ."

Clearly, parents — also Christian parents — differ in their approach to specific child-parent conflicts. Does the Ephesians passage say which of these three parents was "right" and which were "wrong" in the "messy room-movie" conflict? Are there *skills* which parents can use to resolve such conflicts — skills which are based on the kind of Christian love which the Bible recommends for parent-child relations?

This book says "yes" to both questions.

There *is* a set of skills for managing conflicts in the home — skills that really work. Thousands of parents have learned these skills in Parent Effectiveness Training classes, a program developed by Dr. Thomas Gordon, a clinical psychologist. Parents who have learned and use the skills report immediate and tangible results: less fighting, fewer tantrums and lies; warmer feelings and closer relationships; more responsible children.

Moreover, thousands of parents have learned that the PET skills are *congruent with* the Christian faith, as they have participated in Parent Effectiveness classes sponsored by church groups. For example, the special program called Effectiveness Training for Lutherans helps parents see how Christian love (as spelled out in Ephesians) can come alive in a practical set of skills that parents can use in everyday situations of family life.

Purpose of This Book

Dr. Thomas Gordon teaches the PET skills in his book *Parent Effectiveness Training*. In the present book we review the key PET skills, viewing each from the perspective of the Christian faith. Throughout, our concern is to relate *what* a parent does to the crucial considerations of *purpose* (". . . bring them up in the discipline and instruction of the Lord") and *motivation* ("be subject to one another *out of reverence for Christ*").

This book, then, aims to be:

✔ a companion volume for Christian parents who are reading *Parent Effectiveness Training* and/or participating in a PET or church-related PET class. It will help such parents see how the PET skills relate to — and become even more effective as they are powered by — God's love in Christ.

✔ an interest whetter for parents who have not read *Parent Effectiveness Training* and are not enrolled in a PET or church-sponsored parent class. We hope that after reading this book such parents will want to get a fuller description of the PET skills by reading *Parent Effectiveness Training* — or, better yet, by enrolling in a church-sponsored class like ETL (Effectiveness Training for Lutherans). ETL classes supply the book to all participants and also provide further instruction and practice in the skills. The classes are *not* designed to teach the content of the Christian faith. That remains as an important responsibility of the home and the church school. But as this book aims to show, the PET skills do spell out, in practical terms, how Christians can better fulfill their calling to love one another.

— EARL H. GAULKE

Photo by Bob Smith

CHAPTER 1

Starting with You

"Big boys don't cry." Maybe our mother told us this. Or maybe we find ourselves telling our own children something like it. We really mean well when we say it. For we think it's the best way to help the other person; to help him, as we put it, to "control his emotions."

And yet the Bible suggests something entirely different. "Rejoice with those who rejoice and *weep with those who weep!*" (Romans 12:15)

Feelings Are OK

In other words big boys—and even grown men—*may* cry, are even supposed to cry, on occasion. This Bible text affirms —if we take it literally—that it's right and good to have emotions and to express our feelings. And to let others express *their* emotions.

The problem, of course, is that many of us have been trained to suppress or cover up our feelings to a point where we can't know or acknowledge what our true feelings are. And to teach others to suppress their feelings. We say things like: "Don't be afraid. There's nothing to be afraid of." "You shouldn't *laugh* in church!" "You're feeling pain? Be a brave boy and smile."

The popularity of sensitivity groups—and, in many cases, even their excesses—is no doubt due to the impersonality and insensitivity which many experience in their workday and recreational world. People *want* and *need* to feel—and to express their feelings. People want and need to encourage a rich life of feeling in others. For even as God created fish to swim and birds to fly — so, St. Paul would imply, He has created us not only to think, but to feel.

Note first of all, then, how practical and surprising this Biblical principle is in meeting our needs. Practical because it really works. Surprising because it's the opposite of what we might expect. We'd *expect* St. Paul to write, "CHEER UP those who weep. Caution those who are overjoyful that they're in for a fall and that life is not a bowl of cherries."

Look how it works in our everyday relations. Daughter comes home from school, despondent and discouraged.

"What's wrong?" we ask.

"Helen's moving — and now I won't have any friends left at school."

And immediately we move in with: "Oh, sure you will, Honey! You've got *lots* of friends." Or: "Come on, you know you can make all kinds of new friends." Or even: "Don't be such a crybaby! We've all got to learn to live with disappointments."

Such normal reactions — but yet so unhelpful. For they don't really help Mary understand and cope with her feelings of loss.

But notice what happens when we "weep with those who weep." Instead of moving in to oppose and change Mary's mood, we first strive to understand and accept it. And to *show* that we understand by reflecting the feeling: "You're really feeling bad about that. You'll miss Helen."

Such simple words. But when spoken from the heart, they tell Mary that we understand how she feels. They create a bond of closeness rather than alienation. They *support* Mary and help her thus to cope with her feeling of loss.

How dramatically this principle is underscored in the book of Job! Remember how *unhelpful* all the "good advice" of Job's friends was? All their words were worse than futile, for they refused, first of all, to enter into Job's sorrow and to put themselves in his place. And God finally said to them, "My wrath is kindled against you, for you have spoken that which is folly."

Our Basic Problem

Perhaps the problem of Job's friends suggests our basic problem: why we find it difficult to "rejoice with those who rejoice and weep with those who weep." For, like them, we often find ourselves attempting to build up an image of ourselves as people who are capable, unafraid, adequate to all life's challenges. Yet, underneath, we fear that something will happen to make our self-image tumble like a house of cards. We *want* to be a "big boy" (or a big girl), you see; and "big boys" don't cry—even for a friend in need. To do so would show that we are in need as much as he is.

If our child is having trouble making friends, this can threaten our image of ourselves as good and adequate parents —and how can we face up to that?

And so the poison can work through all our relationships. And we end up, at best, treating the other person as a "problem" or as a "case" or as an opportunity to do good—instead of as a person of like passions and failings as ourselves; keeping him at a safe distance from the image of ourselves it seems so desperately important to preserve.

All the time we do this we build up walls instead of bridges between ourselves and people; between ourselves and our own children. We forget the truth of John Donne's words: "Ask not for whom the bell tolls; it tolls for thee." We give up our humanness—our common experience of failings and joys, sorrows and potential to grow—in order to become plaster-cast saints. We forget both the awful truth that we confess *together*, "I, a poor, miserable sinner, confess unto Thee all my sins and iniquities by which I have ever offended

Thee," and the fantastic pardon we receive *together* in Christ: that it doesn't really matter, this business of keeping up a big front, because He loves us and accepts and forgives us despite our sin.

So we need to understand what God is telling us in this simple Bible verse not only in terms of distant sympathy — "feeling with" — but in terms of empathy — "entering into" — the joys and sorrows of people so that they and we might grow as children of God. Sympathy says, "There but for the grace of God go I." You're there — and I'm here, reaching DOWN to you. But empathy says, "What you experience is my experience too. But thank God, His grace is there for both of us."

Jesus Is the Way

This is the point at which our Christian faith makes possible what is impossible in merely psychological therapy. For by faith we know that God Himself — in Christ — didn't simply dish out comforting words and good advice, but *entered into* our condition fully and completely. At Cana's wedding He gives His blessing on our solemn joy and festive fun. In His first miracle at Cana He thus rejoices with those who rejoice. And in His last miracle, the raising of Lazarus, we read that poignant, two-word verse: "Jesus wept." This was no phantom human being; no phony, theatrical tears of a God *dressed up* like man; but true man, God incarnate, entering into our sorrows and joys.

In the words of Hebrews: "Since the children are people of flesh and blood, Jesus Himself became like them and shared their human nature. . . . He had to become like His brothers in every way, in order to be their faithful and merciful High Priest . . . so that the people's sins would be forgiven. And now He can help those who are tempted, because He Himself was tempted and suffered." (Hebrews 2:14-18)

Because He so identified Himself with us, we have become part of His body, His church; so that His own life and love might become alive in us and through us to others.

Forgiveness: The Starting Point

Forgiveness in Christ, then, is the basis for *self*-acceptance — and a growing acceptance of others. In Parent Effectiveness Training, Thomas Gordon speaks of the power of the language of acceptance. "When a person feels that he is truly accepted by another, as he is, then he is freed to move from there and to begin to think about how he wants to change, . . . how he might become more of what he is capable of being. . . . As with the seed, a child contains entirely within his organism the capacity to develop. Acceptance is like the soil — it merely enables the child to actualize his potential."

The language of acceptance, validated in the practice of professional counselors, takes on added dimensions when viewed from the standpoint of our Christian faith. "God shows His love for us in that *while we were yet sinners* Christ died for us. . . . *While we were enemies* we were reconciled to God by the death of His Son" (Romans 5:8-10). Our relationship to God begins with *His accepting us!* In faith, we rely on His acceptance — not because of our goodness, but simply because of His grace. "Just as I am, without one plea but that Thy blood was shed for me and that Thou bid'st me come to Thee. . . ."

Because I'm accepted, I'm free to grow. Contrary to what we might expect, forgiveness means new power to become what God intends us to be. After spelling out, in five chapters, the meaning of God's grace in Christ, St. Paul begins his sixth chapter of Romans with the question: "What shall we say then? Are we to continue in sin that grace may abound? By no means! How shall we who died to sin still live in it? Do you not know that all of us who have been baptized into

15

Christ Jesus were baptized into His death? We were buried therefore with Him by baptism into death, so that as Christ was raised from the dead by the glory of the Father, we too might walk in newness of life." (Romans 6:1-4)

As Martin Luther puts it in his Small Catechism, "In Baptism God forgives sin, delivers from death and the devil, and gives everlasting salvation to all who believe what He has promised." And Baptism means for daily living "that our sinful self, with all its evil deeds and desires should be drowned through daily repentance; and that day after day a new self should arise to live with God in righteousness and purity forever."

Each baptized person — *including our children* — therefore has at work in him the power of God's Spirit to turn from sin to God; the power to "grow to the measure of the stature of the fulness of Christ" (Ephesians 4:7). We *are* alive; we do have within ourselves (in what the Bible calls the "new man" or "spirit") the power to grow in Christ.

Our responsibility as Christian parents is not to "take over" their growth, but to acknowledge the power of God at work in our fellow family members — and to facilitate it.

"Accepted in the Beloved [Jesus Christ], called to be His sons" (Ephesians 1:5, 6), we are called into a family of which Jesus Christ is the Head. Accepted by Him and in Him, we accept one another as members of His body. "Be subject *to one another* out of reverence for Christ" (Ephesians 5:21) is the key verse standing at the beginning of the section in Paul's letter to the Ephesians in which he speaks of family relations. My children are not mine — but His. He created them, redeemed them, sanctifies them. *He* empowers them to grow.

This, of course, runs counter to what many of us have been brought up to believe: "that the best way to help a child become something better in the future is to tell him what you *don't* accept about him now." And so we moralize, evaluate, judge, criticize, and preach at our children. We rely on messages that convey *unacceptance* of the child as he is, feeling that thereby *we* can *force* growth:

"Why do you feel stupid? You know you're very bright.
"You don't feel hungry. We just ate an hour ago.
"Don't be such a crybaby.
"Quit your sulking this minute!"

Who Owns the Problem?

Well, we say, I've got feelings too. And sometimes my child's behavior really bugs me. What about *my* feelings? What about those times when my child's behavior isn't acceptable to me?

Good questions—and important ones. They suggest that we *begin* any process of communication by asking ourselves, in P.E.T. terms, "Who owns the problem?"

Dr. Gordon suggests that we might imagine all the possible behaviors of our child as contained in a window—a window we "see" through:

All
Possible
Behaviors
of Your
Child

We divide this window into two parts: behavior of our child we readily *accept;* behaviors which are *unacceptable* to us:

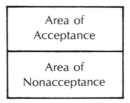

Area of
Acceptance

Area of
Nonacceptance

17

How about locating, right now, some of the behaviors of your child in one area or the other? Draw a window and write them in. (Here are some behaviors that come to my mind: *Top area:* Cheri gives me a hug; Steve rakes the leaves without even being asked; Cheri fixes a surprise lunch; Steve asks me to go bike riding. *Bottom area:* Steve twirls his key chain while we're watching TV; Cheri doesn't return my pen; Steve asks me to repeat what I just said; Cheri's loud record-playing distracts my conversation.)

When my child's behavior is in the bottom area, "below my line," *I* "own the problem," I'm the one who's upset at my child's behavior. Therefore in this situation I need to send a message to let my child know how I feel.

When my child's behavior is acceptable to me, "above my line," there's no problem in the relationship for me. But *he* may own a problem:

> He feels stupid.
> He's frightened.
> He's worried.

So we can further divide the top area into two parts: Child owns a problem; no problem:

Behavior acceptable to me	Child owns problem
	No problem
Behavior unacceptable to me	I own the problem

We need to add two other possibilities to the diagram to complete the picture. (P.E.T. skills for each situation on the diagram are in parentheses.)

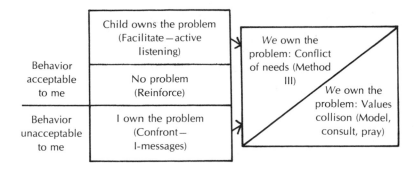

As the diagram shows, there are two kinds of situations in which *"we* own the problem." First of all, there are times when my child's needs and desires are in conflict with my needs and desires:

Child wants to play record player when I want to take a nap.

Child wants to play with me when I need to prepare dinner.

Child needs car for date; I need it to go to a meeting.

In these situations we both "own the problem." My child's behavior, or potential behavior, to satisfy his needs, interferes with my satisfying my needs. And vice versa.

In still another kind of situation in which *we* "own the problem" my child's *values* (what he cherishes and prizes) are in conflict with my values:

Child wants to become social worker. I want him to become an M.D.

Child wants to sleep with teddy bear. I think he's "too old" for this.

Child wants to collect beer cans as a hobby. I feel this is a ridiculous waste of time.

The difference between a conflict of needs and a values collision is readily apparent. In the former, the child's behavior tangibly and concretely interferes with my needs. In the latter, his behavior does not concretely and tangibly affect my meeting my own needs. That's why values conflicts are well described as *collisions*. My efforts to change my child's behavior in these situations will ordinarily be strongly resisted. "It's not hurting you."

In future chapters of this book we'll deal with each of the diagrammed situations in turn. Each calls for a different *kind* of skill. And that's why it's important to keep the diagram in mind. Using skill A in situation B would be like using a saw when a screwdriver is called for. So first identify the situation — *then* use the appropriate skill.

As the diagram shows, P.E.T. suggests that:

When the child "owns the problem," the appropriate skill is one which will facilitate (help) him to solve his *own* problem. That skill is called "active listening."

When there is *no* problem, the appropriate skill is one which reinforces the child's behavior.

When I "own the problem," I need a confronting skill — "I messages."

When *we* own the problem (conflict of needs), we need a problem-solving skill — called "Method III."

When *we* own the problem (values collision), there are three skills that can help: modeling, consulting, prayer.

No doubt most parents would like to move immediately to the third skill, the one to use when "I own the problem." (We will deal with that skill in the next chapter.) However, it's better that we start with the facilitating skill, "active listening," since it must be used *with* "I messages." In a very real sense this first skill, active listening, is the foundation for all the skills which follow it.

Active Listening — and Roadblocks

O.K.? With this overview in mind, let's focus for now only on those situations in which my *child* "owns a problem."

Let's consider two everyday examples of a time when our child might come to us with a problem or with strong feelings of his own. What might you say if your seven-year-old daughter came home crying:

"Mommy, Shirley took my doll! I hate her and I'm never going to play with her again." (You may want to jot down what you'd typically say.)

Next, try this situation. You're reading your evening newspaper. Your 16-year-old son has been pacing around the living room. Suddenly he shouts:

"You're not fair at all! When Robert [older brother] was 16, he could use the car whenever he wanted to. But *I* always have to get in a big hassle before you let *me* use it."

Thomas Gordon classifies the verbal response of many parents to messages like these into twelve categories, the "Typical Twelve" or "dirty dozen." These categories are listed below. About 90% of parental respones fall into the twelve categories.

Scan the list to see where your responses best fit. Then read the entire list, *imagining yourself as the child hearing* each response. How do you feel after you've heard your parents' response? How likely are you (imagining yourself as the child) to modify your behavior — or to change your feeling? (Under each category, the first parental response is to your 7-year-old daughter in the situation given above; the second response is to your 16-year-old son in the using-the-car situation given above.)

1. *Ordering, Directing, Commanding*
   "You go up there and get your doll right back!"
   "Don't you dare talk to me like that!"

2. *Warning, Admonishing, Threatening*
   "If you two can't play better than that, you'll just have to suffer the consequences."
   "One more crack like that, and you'll *never* get to use the car."

3. *Exhorting, Moralizing, Preaching*
   "Pam, don't you know that hating someone is a *sin*?"
   "Children are supposed to *obey* their parents!"

4. *Advising, Giving Solutions or Suggestions*
   "Why don't you talk nicely to Shirley? Then she'll give your doll back."
   "Let me suggest that you give me an advance schedule of your activities."

5. *Lecturing, Teaching, Giving Logical Arguments*
   "If you let Shirley take advantage of you, she'll *always* take your doll away."
   "Responsibility has to be earned."

6. *Judging, Criticizing, Disagreeing, Blaming*
   "I can't believe you weren't partly to blame."
   "Your temper tantrum doesn't change the facts."

7. *Praising, Agreeing*
   "Yes Shirley *is* terrible to be so mean to Mommy's nice little girl."
   "You know, John, you're right. We'll let you use the car whenever you want to."

8. *Name-Calling, Ridiculing, Shaming*
   "You're really being a crybaby, aren't you?"
   "You've certainly got a loud mouth!"

9. *Interpreting, Analyzing, Diagnosing*

'You're just trying to get my sympathy, aren't you?"
"You've always felt jealous of Robert, haven't you?"

10. *Reassuring, Sympathizing, Consoling, Supporting*
    "There, there, it's not so bad!"
    "I used to feel that way when I was your age."

11. *Probing, Questioning, Interrogating*
    "Did you ask her *why* she took your doll?"
    "What makes you think we treat Robert differently from you?"

12. *Withdrawing, Distracting, Humoring, Diverting*
    "How about playing with Susan instead of Shirley?"
    "Let's not talk about it now. Later you'll feel different."

How did you feel—imagining yourself as the *child* hearing each response? Guilty? Inadequate? Put down? Resentful? Powerless or manipulated? Were you more—or less—willing to modify your behavior? More or less capable of solving your own problem?

When psychologists label the "Typical Twelve" responses as "nontherapeutic" or "destructive" of personal growth and heightened interpersonal relationships, their appraisal corresponds with our own personal experience. (Think of the last time you shared your feelings with a friend—and he responded with one of the "Typical Twelve.") We begin to see, too, how they fit into Biblical theology as *misuses of Law and Gospel.*

Distinguishing Law and Gospel

Before we examine that thesis, it may be well to remind ourselves of what we—better, what *God*—means by "Law" and "Gospel." Law and Gospel are the two chief doctrines or teachings of the Bible. The Law reflects God in His holiness —and His will that *we* be holy, as He is. "You shall be holy; for I the Lord, your God, am holy" (Leviticus 19:2). The Law,

23

given by God Himself in the Ten Commandments (Exodus 20) and spelled out in many other sections of the Scriptures, tells us how we are to be and what we are to do and not to do.

The Gospel, on the other hand, reflects God in his love. The Gospel is the good news of our salvation in Jesus Christ. "God so loved the world that he gave His only Son, that whoever believes in Him should not perish but have eternal life." (John 3:16)

Law and Gospel are *alike* in that both are *from God*. Both are equally necessary, for without the Law the Gospel is not understood; without the Gospel the Law benefits us nothing. Both are taught in the entire Bible—Old and New Testaments.

Law and Gospel are *different* in that the Law teaches us what *we* are to do and not to do; the Gospel teaches what *God* has done, and still does, for our salvation. The Law shows us our sin and the wrath of God; the Gospel shows us our Savior and the grace of God. The Law is to be preached to impenitent sinners (including the "flesh" of Christians); the Gospel to those who are troubled and alarmed because of their sins. Most important of all in terms of their power for motivating people: While the Law is a *guide* for Christian behavior, informing us which behaviors are pleasing to God, only the Gospel—NOT THE LAW—can really change and power the Christian person to *do* what the Law requires.

"*Love* is the fulfilling of the Law," writes Paul (Romans 13:10). But how do we come to love God—and His Law? Only through the *Gospel:* "In this is love, not that we loved God but that He loved us and sent His Son to be the expiation for our sins." God's love for us makes possible (though yet imperfectly) our loving people: "Beloved, if God so loved us, we also ought to love one another." (1 John 4:10, 11)

Distinguishing between the Law and the Gospel—knowing what each is for and what it can and cannot do—is of crucial importance in our everyday lives.

"This point of doctrine, namely, the *distinction* between the *Law* and the *Gospel*," writes Luther in his *Commentary on Galatians* (2:3, 4), "we must needs know because it contains *the sum of all Christian teaching*. Let every one who is zealous to be godly strive, then, with the greatest care to learn how to make this distinction not only in his speech, but also in truth and in his experience, that is, in heart and conscience. This distinction is made easily enough in words. But in affliction you will realize that the Gospel is a rare guest in men's consciences, while the Law is their daily and familiar companion."

Through home devotions, participation in the worship service, and through instruction in Christian schools we who are members of a Christian family grow in knowing *what* the Law and Gospel are. We learn the demands of the Law. We are *empowered* by the hearing of the Gospel. We relate to one another as Christians, people who are not "already perfect" but who are on the way "toward the goal . . . of the call of God in Christ Jesus." (Phil. 3:12-14)

What the Law Can't Do

As such, we seek to speak and to surface Gospel power in one another—knowing that only through the Gospel can we and our fellow family members grow. As C. F. W. Walther so aptly puts it, "The Word of God is not rightly divided when an attempt is made, by means of the demands or the threats or the promises of the Law, to induce the unregenerate to put away their sins and engage in good works and thus become godly; on the other hand, when an endeavor is made, by means of the commands of the Law rather than by the admonitions of the Gospel, to urge the regenerate to do good." (*The Proper Distinction Between Law and Gospel*, p. 381)

In other words, the Law—which is indeed God's Law and is therefore holy and just and good—cannot accomplish that which it demands. In fact, when the Law—apart from the

Gospel—is "laid on" people, its effect is not to decrease but to *increase* sin. In Romans 7:7-25 Paul speaks from his own experience of this paradoxical effect of the Law: "Sin [the power of sin within him—and us; our desire to "be right," to justify ourselves, to want to go our own way], *finding opportunity in the commandment,* wrought in me all kinds of covetousness. . . . When the commandment came, *sin revived* . . .; the very commandment which promised life proved to be death to me."

"The *power* of sin is the Law." (1 Cor. 15:56)

C. F. W. Walther well summarizes the effects or outcomes of the Law: "In the first place, . . . the effect of preaching the Law . . . is to increase the lust for sinning. . . . In the second place, the Law uncovers to man his sins, but offers no help to get out of them and thus hurls man into despair." Like a leash put on a mad dog, the Law curbs our outward *expression* of hostility, while *increasing* inner rage. Like a mirror, it shows us our sin in all its ugliness—and leads us to despair.

The Law can, in addition, produce a third effect—contrition, or sorrow over sin. "But if no additional teaching besides the Law [i.e., the Gospel] is applied to man, he must despair, die, and perish in his sins. Ever since the Fall the Law can produce no other effects in man." (Walther)

Use or Misuse of Law? An Example

If we examine the "Typical Twelve" at work in the two parent-child situations we sketched in the foregoing, it becomes apparent that they are all *uses of Law apart from Gospel* —and thus *misuses* likely to produce in our child either resistance and unwillingness or the lessened self-concept that the Bible calls "despair."

Situation 1: Your seven-year-old daughter comes home crying: "Mommy, Shirley took my doll! I hate her and I'm never going to play with her again." When we as parents react to our child in a situation like this simply on the basis of Law, we judge: "It looks like Shirley sinned against my daughter. Taking someone else's property is stealing. Pam is sinning too. Hate is certainly contrary to God's Law that we are to love even our enemies." We evaluate the situation as involving sins against God's Law. And we are probably *right* in this evaluation. But see what's at work as we try to apply Law — apart from Gospel — in responding with the "Typical Twelve."

1. *Ordering* . . . "You go up there and get your doll right back." Seems fair: "An eye for an eye and a tooth for a tooth" (Exodus 21:24). But then there's that word of Jesus: "Do not resist one who is evil. . . . If any one would sue you and take your coat [doll?], let him have your cloak [other playthings?] as well" (Matthew 5:38ff.). Looks like the content of the order doesn't square at all with Christ's Teaching about the Law! How about an order like "Stop fighting!" After all, fighting is against God's Law. Or ordering Pam to tell Shirley, "You've sinned against God's Law!" But then, Pam already *knows* she's "not to fight." Adding *more* Law to her own internalized Law simply adds to her weight of despair. Besides, maybe Pam *didn't* fight. So that order can't help too much. Will telling Shirley "you've sinned," when *Pam* has admitted hate, lead to anything but reciprocal name-calling? Seems like a dead end. Orders don't give any *power* to resolve the conflict. (That's got to come from the Gospel.)

2. *Warning* . . . "If you two can't play better than that, you'll just have to suffer the consequences." This approach squarely points out what Pam is already experiencing: lack of love (on Pam's part? Shirley's? both?) leads to unhappiness. The Law has been spoken. But it doesn't *lead* anywhere. Pam feels the same as before — probably a lot worse. (Again, the despair of the Law.) How about a more "religious" warning, like: "If you don't play better than that, *Jesus* won't love you

27

(Shirley)"? More devastating still—besides being untrue. ("God shows His love for us in that *while we were yet sinners* Christ died for us." Romans 5:8)

3. *Exhorting* . . . "Pam, don't you know that hating someone is a sin?" Correctly, on the basis of the Law, labels sin for what it is. And, in accordance with the function of the Law, will either increase Pam's feelings of hate or lead Pam to despair (Romans 7:7-9). Another dead end.

4. *Advising* . . . "Why don't you talk nicely to Shirley? Then she'll give your doll back." Subtly puts the blame on Pam. ("If you had talked nicely, it wouldn't have happened.") As such, may be resisted, with resentment transferred to the parent.

5. *Lecturing* . . . "If you let Shirley take advantage of you, she'll *always* take your doll away." Similar to number 1, above. The content of the lecture in this example does not measure up to the full requirements of the Law as expressed by Jesus in the Sermon on the Mount. There *is*, of course, a place for *teaching* the Law—in nonstressful situations like home devotions or a religious instructon class. But "laying down the Law" in a stressful situation is counterproductive. It increases resistance to the Law. "When the commandment came, sin revived." (Romans 7:9)

6. *Judging* . . . "I can't believe you weren't partly to blame." "Judging," as defined by Thomas Gordon and illustrated in this response, is really the *judgmentalism* against which the Scriptures speak: "Judge not, and you will not be judged" (Luke 6:37). The response *finds* fault—where no "fault" may in fact be there. If fault *is* there, the "Law" communicated in this response will most likely, again, lead to the resistance, resentment, or despair spoken of in Romans 7:7-9.

7. *Praising* . . . "Yes, Shirley *is* terrible to be so mean to Mommy's little girl." Praises Pam and *judges* (is judgmental of) Shirley. Misuses Law by applying it to Shirley—and not to Pam. May lead to self-righteousness: "I'm better than you."

28

8. *Name-Calling* . . . "You're certainly being a crybaby, aren't you?" Is contrary to Romans 12:15 ". . . weep with those who weep." Judgmental. Likely to lead Pam to despair ("I'm no good"), or to counterattack ("You're a crybaby too") — typical responses to Law.

9. *Interpreting* . . . "You're just trying to get my sympathy, aren't you?" If the interpretation is wrong, Pam feels the resentment of misapplied Law. If it's right, it's felt as an unfair put-down; for, after all, there's nothing *wrong* about wanting sympathy.

10. *Reassuring* . . . "There, there, it's not so bad!" While perhaps *intended* to be supportive, is actually not so. Attempts to *change* the child's feeling without hearing or understanding it. *Real* support and love "weeps with those who weep," entering into the other's feeling.

11. *Probing* . . . "Did you ask her *why* she took your doll?" Conveys a subtle judgmentalism. Doesn't hear Pam's hurt. Thus falls short of loving "your neighbor as yourself."

12. *Withdrawing* . . . "How about playing with Susan instead of Shirley?" Or: "Mommy (Daddy) doesn't have time to talk now." Or: "Work it out for yourself." All of these, as a denial of help, convey the message "I don't care." As such, they fall short of the outgoing love the Law requires.

Another Example

How about the second situation? Your 16-year old son has been pacing around the living room. Suddenly he shouts: "You're not fair at all! When Robert [older brother] was 16, he could use the car whenever he wanted to. But *I* always have to get in a big hassle before you let *me* use it."

This is different from the first situation in that the child's feelings more directly involve us, the parent. It could therefore be "below our line." (If so, we'd want to use the skill outlined in the next chapter.) However, assuming that we don't "buy into" what is essentially *his* problem (he's the one who clearly has feelings of resentment), what might happen in a purely Law approach?

On the basis of the Law, we judge: "This kid is being disrespectful — maybe even disobedient. 'Honor your father and your mother' is God's fourth commandment. 'Children, obey your parents.'"

Chances are that the Law is also judging *me*, the parent, in this situation — though I may be repressing its voice that says: "Hey, he's accusing *me* of not being fair; of loving Robert more. Is that true? He's *angry* — and the Bible *does* say, 'Fathers, do not provoke your children to anger.'" The effects of the Law — if I listen to it only — can thus be that I resist it in a self-defensive anger on my part ("*You're* to blame") or that I despair under its indictment ("You're right. *I'm* to blame.").

Again, analyzing the "Typical Twelve" responses in this situation exposes them as uses, or misuses, of Law apart from Gospel.

1. *Ordering* . . . "Don't you dare talk to me like that!" Seems like self-defensive anger. I hear blame (Law) from my son and I react with blame (Law). My sinful self (the Bible calls this the "old man" — and there's an "old man" in women too) lashes out to hit my son's "old man." The result, according to the predictable effects of the Law, is likely to be either an escalating power struggle — or that my son gives in under the weight of my fury. He stops his "harsh talk," but still feels resentful or put-down.

2. *Warning* . . . "One more crack like that and you'll *never* get to use the car." Effect of this response and its likely dynamics are the same as *Ordering*.

3. *Exhorting* . . . "Children are supposed to *obey* their parents!" Neatly and correctly communicates Law. And, in accordance with the function of the Law, is likely either to increase resistance or lead to merely external compliance.

Also, may be received as further evidence of unfairness in this situation, for my son hasn't actually disobeyed me. Uses Bible as a club. "An endeavor . . . , by means of the commands of the Law rather than by the admonitions of the Gospel, to urge the regenerate to do good." (Walther)

4. *Advising* . . . "Let me suggest that you give me an advance schedule of your activities." Avoids hearing my son's complaint (his "Law" spoken to me), and in this respect becomes *my* evasion of a Law indictment.

5. *Lecturing* . . . "Responsibility has to be earned." Sounds good, but the content of this lecture is neither Biblical nor Christian. "Do good first [be responsible] and then I'll reward you [let you use the car]" turns topsy-turvy the Biblical model: First God loves and forgives us; *then* we are empowered to be "good" — responsible, loving, etc. "We love Him because He first loved us" (1 John 4:19). Again, Law apart from Gospel is likely to be counterproductive.

6. *Judging* . . . "Your temper tantrum doesn't change the facts." Assumes that the parent has correctly interpreted "the facts." Evidences unwillingness (resistance to Law in *my* heart) to hear my son's perhaps "just" complaint. "Judge not and you will not be judged."

7. *Praising, Agreeing* . . . "You know, John, you're right. We'll let you use the car whenever you want to." This one *could* be sincere contrition on my part: John actually is right; I have been unfair; I'm sorry. But "We'll let you use the car whenever you want to" sounds more like the parent giving in to the son's complaint while at the same time feeling resentful about it. Thus doesn't really deal honestly with either his complaint or my felt needs.

8. *Name-Calling* . . . "You've certainly got a loud mouth!" Again, sidesteps hearing my son's feelings or any possibility of there being justice in his complaint. Likely to lead him to

despair ("I'm no good") or to counterattack ("You're a loud mouth too") — typical responses to Law.

9. *Interpreting* . . . "You've always felt jealous of Robert, haven't you?" If the interpretation is wrong, my son feels the resentment of misapplied Law. If it's right, it's felt as a loveless put-down; for, after all, the *feeling* of not being loved (what's underlying the "jealousy") in itself is not sinful (though, to be sure, what one *does* with this feeling may be). In the context of this situation, "jealousy" is branded as wrong, missing entirely that it may simply be a cry for love. (Incidentally, God describes Himself as a "jealous God," Exodus 20:5.)

10. *Reassuring* . . . "I used to feel that way when I was your age." While perhaps intended to be supportive, is actually not so. Puts down my son's feeling as not being too important. Doesn't really *hear* the feeling. Evades the accusation in my son's message.

11. *Probing* . . . "What makes you think we treat Robert different from you?" Denies any blameworthiness on my (the parent's) part. Self-righteous. Subtly judgmental.

12. *Withdrawing* . . . "Let's not talk about it now. Later you'll feel different." As a denial of my son's complaint, conveys the message, "I don't *care* what you're feeling." Falls short of the outgoing love the Law requires.

Listening for Feelings

If the "Typical Twelve" are psychologically and theologically harmful responses, what's left? How can we respond to our child when he "owns a problem"?

Dr. Gordon suggests "simple door-openers," responses which free a child to say more: "I see"; "Tell me more"; "Sounds like you've got something to say about this"; etc. Passive listening, too, often invites the sender to further share his own feelings or problem. Even more effective is "active" listening—the process of *listening for the feelings* that underlie a communication, and *reflecting these back* to the sender as accurately as possible—without additions or without judgments.

To illustrate. Take the situation where our seven-year-old daughter comes home crying: "Mommy, Shirley took my doll! I hate her and I'm never going to play with her again."

Active listening response: "You're really *upset* about what Shirley did. And you're very angry with her."

What effect is a response like that likely to have? For one, it encourages Pam to continue sharing her problem. It conveys acceptance and love. It respects Pam as a person. And it facilitates Pam working through her own problem, in the power God's Spirit provides.

Note how active listening might continue to help Pam define her problem, develop some self-insight, and work toward her own solution:

Pam: Yes, I am upset. Just when we're really having fun, Shirley wants her own way!

Parent: What made it so bad is that you *were* having fun.

Pam: Yes . . . I like to play with Shirley, but I wish she wouldn't get so bossy.

Parent: Sounds like you enjoy some things about Shirley—and you really can't stand some other things.

Pam (thoughtfully): Yeah. . . . I do like her—except when she orders me around. I guess that's why I always go to her house. She's lots more fun than Susan.

Parent: Even though you don't like it when she gets bossy, she's still your favorite friend.

Pam: Yeah. . . . Funny, she says *I'm* the one that's bossy.

Parent: You're wondering: Who's bossy—me or Shirley?

Pam: I guess I am. . . . Whenever we fight, she says I want my way and I say "You want your way." Like today, I wanted to play house and she wanted to play hospital.

Parent: You're really having fun—and then suddenly you don't agree. It's really puzzling, what to do. . . .

Pam: Sometimes she gets her way and sometimes I get my way—and sometimes we fight. Sometimes—I guess we just play.

Parent: It's hard to figure out what makes the difference?

Pam: It sure is hard! I guess sometimes I *am* bossy, like Shirley says. Maybe we're *both* bossy. Maybe if we . . .

Notice how, in this brief exchange, the parent puts aside his (her) own thoughts and feelings and simply endeavors to understand and enter into Pam's thoughts and feelings. The parent recognizes that *Pam* owns the problem and trusts that, as she is enabled to sort out her own feelings, she has the resources to work towards her own solution. Active listening helps Pam to deal with her feelings by ventilating them. It promotes a feeling of warmth between parent and child. It facilitates problem-solving by the child. It enables a parent to really get to know his (her) child—where the child really lives, in her inner thought and emotions. Finally, by *modeling* listening, it influences the child to be more willing to listen to the parents' thoughts and feelings.

Active Listening: Is It Biblical?

The attitude behind active listening—and active listening itself—draws clear support from the Scriptures. "A soft answer turns away wrath" (Proverbs 15:1). St. James advises: "Let every man be quick to hear, slow to speak" (1:19). St. Paul, as we previously cited, invites the Roman Christians to "rejoice with those who rejoice and weep with those who weep." (Romans 12:15)

Active-listening to our child in his problems takes seriously the doctrine of the new birth in Christ, recognizing that our child has *within himself,* in his "new man" (Galatians 5,

Romans 7) the power to change. Original sin ("old man") manifests itself when *we* don't *want* to hear the other person's hurts.

Each person in our families both stands by himself before God and, when redeemed, is called to minister to — to facilitate and free — his fellow member in the family of Christ. "Work out your own salvation" (Philippians 2:12) supports the stance of letting the other "own" his own problem, recognizing that "*God* is at work in you, both to will and to work for His good pleasure." (v. 13)

The kind of empathic love that underlies active listening — seeing the other as *apart* from us, as a unique individual, while at the same time identifying with him in his problems and feelings — is described in those parodoxical verses in Galatians 6:2, 5: "Bear one another's burdens, and so fulfill the law of Christ. . . . For each man will have to bear his own load." Hearing, not squelching, the other's feelings by active listening facilitates the other's "handling" his feelings in the power that God's Spirit supplies to him.

The Word — God Himself in Christ — became flesh, entering into and experiencing all the sorrows and joys and hurts of our human condition — of *my* human condition. That's a fact that makes me feel warm. Maybe even warm enough to get close to my child — close enough to hear and identify with his hurts — all the while letting him be the separate person in whom Christ is Himself at work.

Active listening, then, a skill to use *when your* child *owns the problem,* can be an effective way to "love one another as I have loved you."

Photo by Ron Sievert

CHAPTER 2

Say It with Love

Parents are people too. They have needs, problems, feelings. There are times when a child's behavior is clearly unacceptable to you, the parent. His behavior tangibly affects you:

Pam fixes an after-school snack and leaves a mess in the kitchen.

Steve tinkers with his bike — and leaves the screwdriver rusting in the driveway.

Cheri keeps interrupting you when you're talking on the phone.

Dave runs the car out of gas and you're late for work.

Scott doesn't clean his gerbil cage, and the stink is driving you out of your mind.

In situations like these, the parent's needs are not being met. The *parent* "owns" the problem. What can a parent do to modify the child's unacceptable behavior?

Let's take a specific example: You're working on your income tax. You just have time to finish it before the deadline, and need to concentrate. Your eight-year-old son is listening to a TV program in the next room — a program his teacher told him to watch. The TV volume seems awfully loud and is beginning to annoy you more and more. So you say . . .

1. "Turn off the TV this minute!" *(ordering)*

2. "If you don't turn down the TV, I'll come and do it for you." *(warning)*

3. "Hey, can't you be more considerate?" *(exhorting)*

4. "Why don't you go listen at David's house?" *(advising)*

"You Messages": Judgmental Put-Downs

These four of the "Typical Twelve" communicate *your* solution of the problem, leaving the child out of it. They convey little or no recognition of his needs. As Law-oriented power statements, they may well lead the child to defensiveness or to feelings of being "put down." They don't free him to act responsibly, out of consideration for your needs.

More direct put-downs are represented by roadblocks 5, 6, 8, and 9, messages that could easily be given in this situation:

5. "How would you like it if I did that to you?" (*"teaching"*)

6. "You're certainly being inconsiderate." (*judging*)

8. "Hey, Dummy, how about turning the TV up a little so all of us can go deaf?" (*name-calling*)

9. "Are you trying to get even with me for something that's bugging you?" (*interpreting*)

Put-down messages, as judgmental messages of Law apart from Gospel love, are likely to lead to the child's feeling guilty — and powerless and condemned in that guilt (the despair which the Law works); or to lead to resistance and a Law-oriented power struggle: "You're not so considerate yourself!" "I didn't do anything wrong!" "Why don't you move if the TV's bothering you?"

"I Messages": Loving Confrontation

By contrast, telling the child *how you feel*—with a non-blameful description of the behavior which is interfering with your needs —

✔ is nonjudgmental.

✔ conveys your trust in him as a person who is a child of God and is empowered by God's Spirit.

✔ frees him to respond to your need in the power of his "new man" — willingly, out of love.

38

✔ facilitates your child's growth in the new life in Christ — the life which relates constructively to others in love.

"Hey, John, I'm getting kind of panicky. I need to finish this income tax and the loud TV volume is distracting me."

Note that this statement is an "I" message—"I need," "I feel"—rather than a "you" message, like the "Typical Twelve." The nonblameful description of the behavior (an important part of an "I message") clearly identifies the nature of the problem: The *problem* is the loud TV volume. By contrast, "You're being inconsiderate," "You're a dummy," really are unclear communication. They locate the problem inside the child, rather than in the loud TV volume and Dad's need. The child hears "I'm bad" rather than "Dad's upset." And so he is cued to dealing with his feelings of "badness" rather than with the real problem: Dad's feelings and the loud TV.

Note, too, that an "I" message is a far cry from the "permissive" stance that could be communicated by roadblocks 7 (praising), 10 (reassuring), 11 (probing), or 12 (withdrawing). It's difficult to imagine Dad's using praising, reassuring, or probing in the TV situation, unless he became incredibly phony: "John, my dear son, you're such a good boy. Daddy would like it if you turned down the TV." Withdrawing by putting up with the problem leaves Dad with seething resentment. Humoring (a form of withdrawing) is equally inappropriate—and likely not to be congruent with Dad's feelings: "Hey, Johnny, wouldn't I look funny wearing earmuffs?"

An "I message"—effective when you, the parent, own the problem—neither submerges nor represses your need in permissiveness, nor does it convert that need into blameful judging. It transparently communicates your need, with a high probability of leading your child to change his behavior while at the same time maintaining a good relationship with him.

In the TV situation, Dad's "I statement" enables John to

act as a maturing Christian adult. In the "freedom with which Christ has made us free" he can choose (rather than being coerced to act) to meet Dad's need in a number of ways — turning down the volume, going next door to David's house, moving the set, etc. All of these solutions of *his* meet Dad's need. And in a small but measurable amount he is led to grow. Multiply this incident by the hundreds of times that needs conflict in a home — and the growth through "I messages" rather than "you messages" can indeed be significant.

Using "I Messages" with Active Listening

Sometimes, of course, even a clear "I message" will not lead a child to change his behavior:

Dad: I'm really upset about not finding my tools when I need them. When you use my tools and don't put them away, I lose a lot of time hunting for them.

Son: Oh, you're always so fussy with your tools. I was working on my bike and just didn't have time to put them away.

At this point Dad needs to hear the child's feeling; to actively listen, as well as to send another, perhaps stronger, "I message."

Dad: You were pretty absorbed in working on your bike and feel I'm *overly* protective of my tools. Maybe you're right — and we can talk about that. But I sure get very frustrated when I've got a repair job to do and first have to go looking for the screwdrivers.

In this situation, Dad's initial "I message" gave the child a problem. But his active-listening to his son's feelings *while repeating his own* concern communicated acceptance. "Dad hears *me*. I want to deal constructively with *his* feelings."

So "I messages" and "active listening" work in tandem fashion, communicating our *need* while at the same time respecting our child's needs and feelings. If "I messages" coupled with "active listening" don't seem to work in modifying our child's behavior, chances are that there is a "conflict of needs" situation — a subject we will deal with in the next chapter.

"I Messages" and Christian Admonition

But before we move on, it may be well to see more clearly how active listening and "I statements" spell out a *way* to carry out the many passages of Scripture which speak of Christian admonition. Take, for example, Galatians 6:1-2: "Brethren, if a man is overtaken in any trespass, you who are spiritual should restore him in a spirit of gentleness. Look to yourself, lest you too be tempted. Bear one another's burdens, and so fulfill the law of Christ."

That "spirit of gentleness" would seem to be a different spirit from the one underlying "you statements" — the roadblocks of ordering, warning, exhorting, advising, lecturing, judging, and name-calling.

"Look to yourself, lest you too be tempted." When trying to "restore" (rather than demolish) our fellow Christian, our Christian child, we need to recognize that our hurt, our fear, our anger (emotions not sinful in themselves) *can* begin to drive our sinful flesh. They can become transmuted into hate, spite, a spirit of revenge. "For from within, out of the heart of man," says Jesus, "come evil thoughts, fornication, theft, murder, adultery, licentiousness, envy, slander, pride, foolishness" (Mark 7:21-22). When we let our anger become transmuted into hate ("I'd like to wring his neck"), hateful words, and put-down messages, we fail to "look to ourselves" and fall prey to the same sin we're trying to "correct" in the other person.

Yet we are called to "restore" our fellow Christian. Neither

41

angry words ("you statements") nor repressing our feelings is likely to accomplish that purpose. *Sharing* our feelings in an "I statement" communicates a "spirit of gentleness," a recognition that I too might be "at fault," and so fulfills the "law of Christ," communicating genuine Christian love.

Is this irresponsible permissiveness? An evasion of a proper use of the Law? On the contrary, because an "I message" enables me *nonblamefully* to describe my Christian child's behavior, it helps him recognize his own sin. It thus surfaces Law in him *in an evangelical* (Gospel-oriented) *way,* working in Him not a defensive wrath (Romans 7:8) but a godly repentance as he also "hears" the love which underlies the Gospel.

By contrast (as we considered earlier), judging and "preaching at" are actually misuses of Law. As Christians, we want to use the Law to prepare for the Gospel — to "win" rather than to turn away our Christian brother. "I statements" are congruent with Christian love and support our speaking of Gospel. ("It's O.K. God forgives me. And he forgives you too. Isn't Jesus wonderful?") They enable *confrontation* without *condemnation.*

"You have heard that it was said to the men of old. 'You shall not kill; and whoever kills shall be liable to judgment.' But I say to you that every one who is angry [not the *feeling* of anger in itself, for Jesus Himself experienced that feeling, Mark 3:5; rather, the *feeding* of one's own anger — escalating it into hate and resentment] with his brother shall be liable to judgment; whoever insults his brother shall be liable to the council, and whoever says, 'You fool!' shall be liable to the hell of fire. So if you are offering your gift at the altar, and there remember that your brother has something against you, leave your gift there before the altar and go; first be reconciled to your brother, and then come and offer your gift. Make friends quickly with your accuser, while you are going with him to court, lest your accuser hand you over to the judge, and the judge to the guard, and you be put in prison." (Matthew 5:21-25)

It's interesting to note how Paul begins his letters to Christians of his day, among whom were some who needed to be admonished. "To all God's beloved in Rome, who are called to be saints. . . ." "To the church of God which is at Corinth, to those sanctified in Christ Jesus, called to be saints. . . ." "To the saints who are also faithful in Christ Jesus. . . ."

He begins by recognizing who they are — people not holy in themselves, but "saints," holy, forgiven people, through Christ. *Then* he admonishes, not by judgmental put-downs but with a confession of his own inadequacies and an affirmation that "by the grace of God I am what I am." With an "I statement" he confronts the Galatian Christians: "I am astonished that you are so quickly deserting Him who called you in the grace of Christ." He confesses his own former persecution of the church (Galatians 1:13). *What* he says to the Galatians ("For in Christ Jesus you are all sons of God *through faith*," not the Law) he communicates in a transparently personal way, sharing his own feelings about their backsliding: "*I am afraid* I have labored over you in vain." "I could wish to be present with you now and to change my tone, for I am perplexed about you."

What Paul wrote by inspiration of God about the bondage of Law and the freedom which the Gospel brings serves to instruct also contemporary Christians. *How* he related to Christians needing admonition similarly serves as a model for us as we relate person-to-person to our "closest" Christians, the members of our family.

Active-listening to our children when they "own the problem"; confronting them in an evangelical way when we "own the problem": These can do much to expand that "no problem" area (remember the diagram, p.18,19) in our relationships

43

with our children. As a result, there will be more time for mutually enjoyed activities — and more joy in those activities.

Praise: Is It Christian?

What about that "no problem" area? We mentioned in chapter 1 that there is another skill — a "reinforcing" skill — that can enhance relationships in those situations where our child's behavior is *very acceptable* to us:

Without being asked, Steve rakes the leaves in the backyard.

We've returned from an exhausting Saturday shopping trip and discover that Cheri's prepared a "surprise lunch" all ready to eat.

A neighbor tells us, "I really enjoy your kids. They're so friendly and outgoing! Last week Steve helped me carry up my garbage can."

Pam draws a picture "just for you" and gives me a big hug. "I love you, Daddy."

Wow! We really feel warm inside. So we say —

"You're a good boy!" Or —

"Hey, you're a good cook!" Or —

"I really feel *good* when I see the yard so clean. It'll save me a lot of work tomorrow." Or —

"I love you too!" (with a big hug in return)

Well, how would *you* feel if *you* were the child and received each of the above responses? Which would feel good to you? Which would give you a sense of freedom — or a sense of restraint — to repeat your behavior? Imagine yourself as the child, and run through those four responses again. . . .

If, imagining yourself as the child, you felt uncomfortable with the first two responses, you've validated for yourself the negative effects that *praise* can have on a child — even in the "no problem" area. For that's really what the first two responses are. The "problem" with praise is that:

✔ If it doesn't fit with a child's self-image, it may cause him discomfort. (Cheri may *not* think of herself as a "good cook." She may just have wanted to do something helpful for her parent. Steve knows he's not always a "good boy." Besides, it's not what we *do* that makes us "good." That turns topsy-turvy the relationship between faith and works—and leads to self-righteousness.)

✔ It binds rather than frees the child. A child can get "hooked" on praise. If it isn't forthcoming, he wonders what he did wrong: "Last week you praised me. This week you didn't. How come?" *Depending* on the praise of parents fosters *outer*—rather than inner, spiritual—motivation. It may lead to a child who "goes along with the gang," who caves in under peer pressure. (See John 12:43 and Romans 2:29, which contrast the "praise of men" with the "praise" that comes from God.)

✔ A child can interpret praise as a manipulative device of the parent to get him to do what the parent wants. (And he may be right in this interpretation!) "I wonder why Mom said that? She's praising me just because she wants me to keep on doing what *she* wants."

In short, even when there's "no problem," praise is still likely to be a roadblock. For even though it's a positive evaluation, it's still an evaluation, a *judgment*—and as such can convey all the negative effects of Law: defensiveness, resistance, possibly even a lowered self concept. ("Why does she call me a good cook? I don't feel that I am.")

Thanking God, Warming People

In contrast to praise, the last two responses suggested above are not an evaluation of the child, but simply a *sharing of our warm feelings*. And both responses turn out to be "I messages" rather than "you messages."

"*I* feel *good*" about what you did. And I may also share the "why," the concrete and tangible effect: "It'll save me a lot of work tomorrow." Or: "It's really a nice surprise to have a lunch all ready when I'm tired from shopping."

And, of course, that hug says "I love you" better than a lot of words.

Note the following beneficial effects of an "I message" when there's "no problem":

✔ The child is not presented with the problem of checking out a "praise" evaluation with his own self-concept. The message simply shares: "Dad (Mom) feels good." And the shared warmth is likely to make the child "feel good," closer to his parents.

✔ It frees the child to repeat the behavior again out of inner, spiritual motivation rather than outer constraint (desire for praise). In this respect, a genuinely spoken "I message" recognizes that a child's "good work" is a *fruit* of faith, whereas "praise" may well imply that a child's "good work" is a work of Law. (Galatians 3:2; Galatians 5)

It's really true, you see: "It is the God who said, 'Let light shine out of darkness,' who has shone in our hearts to give the light of the knowledge of the glory of God in the face of Christ" (2 Cor. 4:6). Behind—rather, *in*—that gapped-tooth smile of my son I see *Jesus* smiling at me. That warm hug of my daughter feels like—(strange but true) a heavenly Father's love.

No wonder Paul writes, "I thank *my God* through Jesus Christ for all of you. . . ." (Romans 1:8)

He's the one we praise for those "fruits of the Spirit" in our children, our wife/husband. "For the fruit of the Spirit is love, joy, peace, patience, kindness, goodness, faithfulness, gentleness, self-control." (Galatians 5)

CHAPTER 3

Everyone Can Win:
Handling Conflicts

Conflicts. Every family has them. In the very first family Cain killed his brother Abel. Abraham and his wife argued about their sons Ishmael and Isaac. In Isaac's family both parents and children contended about the birthright. And the conflict resulted in Jacob's leaving home. In Jacob's family, when Joseph's brothers "saw that their father loved him more than all his brothers, they hated him and could not speak peaceably to him" (Genesis 37:4). And one day they sold him into slavery. Miriam and Aaron quarreled with their brother Moses (Numbers 12). David's son Absalom tried to take his father's throne away.

Not even the family of Jesus escaped conflict. Mary confronted the boy Jesus in the temple: "Son, why have You treated us so? Behold, Your father and I have been looking for You anxiously."

The "family" of Jesus, the twelve disciples, experienced plenty of conflict among themselves. "And an argument arose among them as to which of them was the greatest" (Luke 9:46). "A dispute also arose among them, which of them was to be regarded as the greatest." (Luke 22:24)

In the early church "the Hellenists murmured against the Hebrews because their widows were neglected in the daily distribution." In Antioch Paul contended with Peter (Galatians 2:11ff.). In Corinth the church experienced factionalism and divisions in the midst of their fellowship meals and their

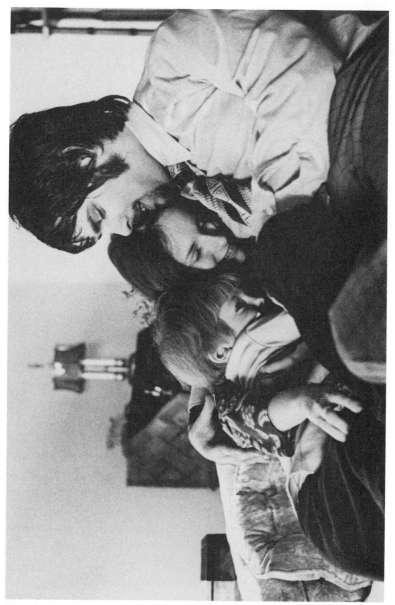

Photo by Bob Combs

celebration of the Lord's Supper (1 Corinthians 11:17ff.).

Conflicts, then, seem to be inevitable also in Christian communities, in Christian homes!

Steve continues to leave dirty dishes in the sink even though his parents have continually confronted him with "I messages."

Lisa dawdles in the morning and keeps on missing the school bus despite Mother's pleas.

Arguments keep breaking out at the dinner table.

In situations like these, we find ourselves in a *conflict of needs* with our children. In this chapter we focus on conflicts of needs, reserving the other kind of conflict (values collisions) for the next chapter. (It might be helpful at this point for the reader to refer back to the diagram and definition of these two kinds of conflicts on page 19.)

Conflicts: Who Should Win?

What can we do when our needs conflict with our child's needs? We can, first of all, recognize that conflicts are inevitable — and that they need not necessarily be *bad*. Not the conflict itself, but *how the conflict is resolved*, is the important consideration. Conflicts can lead to growth, to enhanced interpersonal relationships (as in the case of the boy Jesus in the temple and Paul at Corinth) — or they can lead to strains in or even the destruction of relationships (as in the case of Cain and Abel or David and Absalom). When conflicts are surfaced — and dealt with openly — rather than kept submerged, children learn how to deal with conflicts constructively.

How can a conflict be resolved? If my needs or desires conflict with the needs of my child, it seems apparent that either he must "win" or I must "win." Either he must give in or I must give in.

This way of looking at conflict resolution leads inevitably to a power struggle:

"When it's time for bed, Tommy delays and delays and makes all kinds of excuses. So I just pick him up and put him in bed—no *ifs*, *ands*, or *buts*." The parent uses power to *win* —and the child loses.

Or: "When it's time for bed, Tommy puts up such a fuss that I finally just give in. It bothers me, and I just hate him for it, but what can you do?" The child uses power to win— and the parent loses.

In *Parent Effectiveness Training* Thomas Gordon labels the first option as "Method I" or the "authoritarian" way of resolving conflicts. The parent wins—the child loses. He labels the second option as "Method II" or the "permissive" way of resolving conflicts. In this method the child wins and the parent loses.

Most parents get locked into Method I. Some parents typically prefer Method II. And still other parents vacillate between both methods.

Dr. Gordon presents the following illustration of Method I and II in action:

Jane: 'Bye, I'm off to school.

Parent: Honey, it's raining and you don't have your raincoat on.

Jane: I don't need it.

Parent: You don't need it! You'll get wet and ruin your clothes or catch a cold.

Jane: It's not raining that hard.

Parent: It is too.

Jane: Well, I don't want to wear a raincoat. I hate to wear a raincoat.

Parent: Now, honey, you know you'll be warmer and drier if you wear it. Please go get it.

Jane: I hate that raincoat—I won't wear it!

Parent: You march right back to your room and get that raincoat! I will not let you go to school without your raincoat on a day like this.

50

Jane: But I don't like it. . . .

Parent: No *buts*—if you don't wear it your mother and I will have to ground you.

Jane (angrily): All right, you win! I'll wear the stupid raincoat!

The father got his way. His solution—that Jane wear her raincoat—prevailed, although Jane did not want to. *The parent won and Jane lost.* Jane was not at all happy with the solution, but she surrendered in the face of her parent's threat to use power (punishment).

Here is how Method II operates in parent-child conflicts:

Parent and child encounter a conflict-of-needs situation. The parent may or may not have a preconceived solution. If he does, he may try to persuade the child to accept it. It becomes obvious that the child has his own solution and is attempting to persuade the parent to accept it. If the parent resists, the child might then try to use his power to get compliance from the parent. In the end the parent gives in.

In the raincoat conflict Method II would work like this:

Jane: 'Bye. I'm off to school.

Parent: Honey, it's raining and you don't have your raincoat on.

Jane: I don't need it.

Parent: You don't need it! You'll get wet and ruin your clothes or catch a cold.

Jane: It's not raining that hard.

Parent: It is too.

Jane: Well, I don't want to wear a raincoat. I hate to wear a raincoat.

Parent: I want you to.

Jane: I hate that raincoat—I won't wear it. If you make me wear it, I'll be mad at you.

Parent: Oh, I give up! Go on to school without your raincoat, I don't want to argue with you anymore—you win.

Jane was able to get her own way—she won and her parents lost. The parent certainly was not happy with the solution, yet he surrendered in the face of Jane's threat to use her power (in this case, being mad at her father).*

Negative Consequences of Methods I and II

Although the outcomes are entirely different, both Method I and Method II are alike in that in both each person wants *his* way—and fights to get it. Both involve a struggle in which power (force) is the key element. In Method I, I, the parent, use power to win over the child. In Method II, I give up my power and give in to my child's power. I lose—he wins.

As the two foregoing illustrations show, both methods have serious consequences. When I win over my child (Method I), he is likely to be resentful and to have low motivation to carry out my solution. In addition, I may have to police my solution—continue to monitor his behavior to see that he complies. On a long-term basis, I don't help him to develop *self*-discipline. Fear of punishment or of disapproval is the motivation I'm building on—basically a Law-oriented approach, devoid of Gospel.

In terms of spiritual nurture, then, Method I falls short of the Biblical ideal. *It is a misuse of God's Law.* "The attempt to make men godly by means of the Law and to induce even those who are already believers in Christ to do good by the Law and issuing commands to them, is a very gross confounding of Law and Gospel," writes C. F. W. Walther.

"But isn't Method I the way to teach my children to be obedient?"

As Walther aptly points out, "Forced obedience simply is no obedience." The Law indeed "may accomplish this much, that on account of it we quit this or that vice, but it cannot change our heart." And that, of course, is the somber limitation of the Law.

Similarly, Method II has serious negative consequences — both from a psychological and a spiritual point of view. Children who grow up under a heavy dose of Method II are likely to be impulsive, rude, unmanageable — wise in ways of using power over others: temper tantrums, sulking, bullying, and the like. Method II children are getters, not givers. Thus they are likely to have trouble in establishing relationships with peers and teachers. Not only their parents, but others, will react to them with resentment.

Moreover, parents who rely on Method II feel like doormats. "Poor me" feelings alternate with feelings of anger and resentment at their children. When these parents see the loveless, selfish personalities of their children, they feel guilty over their failure as Christian parents. They judge — and rightly so — that their child's lawlessness and selfishness are poor fruits of faith.

What the Bible Says About Methods I and II

The strange thing is that both Method I and Method II parents can point to Scriptural texts which seemingly support their positions. Method I parents may quote — sometimes to their child in the midst of a conflict: "Children, obey your parents" (Ephesians 6:1) or "Honor your father and your mother" (Exodus 20:12). The problem is that when parents thus use these texts *as arguments to buttress their power*, the children may just as validly use counter-texts to support *their* use of power: "Fathers, do not provoke your children to anger" (Ephesians 6:4). "You're supposed to 'love your neighbor — even kids — as yourself.' How would you like it if I forced you to do what you want me to do?"

And, of course, both parents and children are right — and wrong — in such appeals to Scripture. They're *right* in pointing out that God does delineate a blueprint for parent-child relationships. They're *wrong* in using Scripture to support a basically power stance. In quoting Scripture to support their own position, they fail to see that Scripture as *Law* always speaks to *me,* not the other person. And so, in the midst of a conflict, the word of Scripture to *me,* the parent, is "Fathers, provoke not your children to wrath," even as the word of Scripture to the child is "Children, obey your parents." By applying the Law to the *other* person rather than to ourselves, we grossly misuse Law—and inevitably find ourselves in escalating power struggles, with neither person in the final analysis "winning."

Christian parents and children need therefore to note the important qualifying phrases added to the above texts. "Children, obey your parents *in the Lord. . . .*" "Fathers, do not provoke your children to anger, but bring them up in the discipline and instruction *of the Lord.*"

Christian family life is not a matter of parent power vs. child power—with one losing, the other winning. Rather it's a relationship to one another *in Christ.* The key verse, introducing the so-called "Table of (Family) Duties" in Ephesians, clearly states: *"Be subject to one another out of reverence for Christ."* The power that lords it over the fellow member of the family becomes unnecessary as we practice the inner power that the Gospel gives: "Husbands, love your wives, *as Christ loved the church* and gave Himself up for her. . . ." (Ephesians 5:25)

"A More Excellent Way"

One possible reason that we cling to Method I—the authoritarian or "my power" method—is that we confuse *authoritarianism* with *authority.* Yet Jesus speaks of "authority" —genuine, Christ-like authority—not in terms of *power*

54

(authoritarianism), but in terms of *service* to the fellow-Christian.

He explained the matter quite clearly to His disciples one day. "Then the mother of the sons of Zebedee came up to Him, with her sons, and kneeling before Him she asked Him for something. And He said to her, 'What do you want?' She said to Him, 'Command that these two sons of mine might sit, one at Your right hand and one at Your left, in Your kingdom.' . . . And when the ten heard it, they were indignant at the two brothers. But Jesus called them to Him and said, 'You know that the rulers of the Gentiles lord it over them, and their great men exercise authority over them. *It shall not be so among you;* but whoever would be great among you must be your servant, and whoever would be first among you must be your slave; even as the Son of Man came not to be served, but to serve and to give His life as a ransom for many.' " (Matthew 20:20-28)

Remember how Jesus demonstrated this concept of authority? In an upper room, when no servant was present to wash feet that were begrimed with the dust of the road, Jesus "rose from supper, laid aside His garments, and girded Himself with a towel. Then He poured water into a basin and began to wash the disciples' feet and to wipe them with the towel with which He was girded. . . ."

This word and action of Jesus illustrates the phrases sprinkled through the Table of Duties in Ephesians 5 and 6: ". . . in the Lord," "as Christ loved the church," ". . . as to Christ." The "authority" given to parents means that we are called to exercise *responsibility* to help our children and our wife (husband) *to grow in their life in Christ,* that the church in our house might one day "be presented before Him in splendor, without spot or wrinkle or any such thing, that she might be holy and without blemish."

The Scriptures assert, then, that there *is* a third alternative

55

to Methods I and II. Through the words of Paul, God says, "I will show you a still more excellent way." And those words introduce the marvelous thirteenth chapter of 1 Corinthians, the chapter which spells out the dynamic of Christian love in action: "Love is patient and kind; love is not jealous or boastful; it is not arrogant or rude. Love does not insist on its own way, it is not irritable or resentful; it does not rejoice at wrong, but rejoices in the right. Love bears all things, believes all things, hopes all things, endures all things."

The "better way," the way which takes seriously, *"Be subject to one another out of reverence for Christ,"* discards parental power (Method I) even as it refuses to buckle under child power (Method II). Instead of "you vs. me" it seeks solutions to conflict in terms of "we" — together in Christ.

For Christian parents who seek to put into practice this Biblical model, Thomas Gordon's description of Method III (the "no lose" method of resolving conflict) has a lot to offer. Here's his description and illustration of Method III in action:

> Parent and child encounter a conflict-of-needs situation. The parent asks the child to participate with him in a joint search for some solution acceptable to both. One or both may offer possible solutions. They critically evaluate them and eventually make a decision on a final solution acceptable to both. No selling of the other is required after the solution has been selected, because both have already accepted it. No power is required to force compliance, because neither is resisting the decision.
>
> Bringing back our familiar raincoat problem, here is how it was resolved by Method III, as reported by the parent involved:
>
> *Jane:* 'Bye, I'm off to school.
> *Parent:* Honey, it's raining outside and you don't have your raincoat on.
> *Jane:* I don't need it.
> *Parent:* I think it's raining quite hard and I'm concerned

that you'll ruin your clothers or get a cold, and that will affect us.

Jane: Well, I don't want to wear my raincoat.

Parent: You sure sound like you definitely don't want to wear that raincoat.

Jane: That's right, I hate it.

Parent: You really hate your raincoat.

Jane: Yeah, it's plaid.

Parent: Something about plaid raincoats you hate, huh?

Jane: Yes, nobody at school wears plaid raincoats.

Parent: You don't want to be the only one wearing something different.

Jane: I sure don't. Everybody wears plain-colored raincoats — either white or blue or green.

Parent: I see. Well, we really have a conflict here. You don't want to wear your raincoat 'cause it's plaid, but I sure don't want to pay a cleaning bill, and I will not feel comfortable with you getting a cold. Can you think of a solution that we both could accept? How could we solve this so we're both happy?

Jane: (pause) Maybe I could borrow Mom's car coat today.

Parent: What does that look like? Is it plain-colored?

Jane: Yeah, it's white.

Parent: Think she'll let you wear it today?

Jane: I'll ask her. (Comes back in a few minutes with car coat on; sleeves are too long, but she rolls them back.) It's okay by Mom.

Parent: You're happy with that thing?

Jane: Sure, it's fine.

Parent: Well, I'm convinced it will keep you dry. So if you're happy with that solution, I am too.

Jane: Well, so long.

Parent: So long. Have a good day at school.*

Notice how no power was involved in this interchange. The parent, using "I messages," confronted the child with his needs. Through active listening, he heard the child's needs. Then both sought a solution acceptable to both. The result: The conflict was resolved with no one losing. And Jane and Father felt good about each other.

Positive Consequences of Method III

Psychologically, Method III is more effective than Methods I or II because:

✔ The child is involved in the solution process—and so is more highly motivated to carry it out. (Little or no policing of the solution is necessary.)

✔ Instead of just two solutions (my power solution and the child's), a variety of creative solutions will be considered. Thus, there is a much higher probability of finding a solution that is really satisfying to both parent and child.

✔ Children's thinking skills are sharpened.

✔ Relationships are enhanced as each person demonstrates his willingness to meet the other's needs.

✔ The real problem, rather than surface symptoms, are surfaced. (In the raincoat situation, Methods I and II get stuck on the question of "who wins" without uncovering the real concern of Jane—that she be in step with her peers.)

In terms of spiritual nurture, Method III is preferable to Methods I and II because:

✔ It respects the child as a person who, while not perfect, has within himself (in his "new man") the will to meet his parents' needs in love.

✔ It puts into practice Christian love: "Love does not insist on its own way." "Be subject to one another out of reverence for Christ."

✔ It replaces the power which lords it over the other (authoritarianism) with the genuine authority which Christ gives to parents: the authority of leading and feeding, rather than forcing.

Speaking "New Man" to "New Man"

Another way of analyzing what happens in Methods I, II, and III is to see it in terms of the Biblical dynamic of Romans 7:18ff. and Galatians 5:16ff. In these two Scripture selections Paul speaks of another conflict—a conflict within each Christian:

> I do not understand my own actions. For I do not do what I want, but I do the very thing I hate. Now if I do not do what I want, I agree that the Law is good. So then it is no longer I that do it, but sin which dwells within me. For I know that nothing good dwells within me, that is, in my flesh. I can will what is right, but I cannot do it. For I do not do the good I want, but the evil I do not want is what I do. Now if I do what I do not want, it is no longer I that do it, but sin which dwells within me.
>
> So I find it to be a law [a general principle] that when I want to do good, evil lies close at hand. For I delight in the Law of God, in my inmost self, but I see in my members another law at war with the law of my mind and making me captive to the law of sin which dwells in my members. Wretched man that I am! Who will deliver me from this body of death? Thanks be to God through Jesus Christ our Lord! So then, I of myself serve the Law of God with my mind, but with my flesh I serve the law of sin. (Romans 7:15-25)
>
> For you were called to freedom, brethren; only do not use your freedom as an opportunity for the flesh, but through love be servants of one another. For the whole Law is fulfilled in one word, "You shall love your neighbor as yourself." But if you bite and devour one another take heed that you are not consumed by one another.

But I say, walk by the Spirit and do not gratify the desires of the flesh. For the desires of the flesh are against the Spirit, and the desires of the Spirit are against the flesh; for these are opposed to each other, to prevent you from doing what you would. But if you are led by the Spirit you are not under the Law. (Galatians 5:13-18)

Put on the new man. . . . (Ephesians 4:24; Colossians 3:10)

According to Biblical psychology, then, a Christian is, at the same time (in Luther's words), both a sinner and a saint. The inmost "I," the "reborn" part of me, is in touch with God's Spirit and "delights in the Law of God." Part of me wants to—and, led by the Spirit, is *able* to—love my neighbor as myself.

But another part of me—the "flesh," the "law at work in my members," "indwelling sin"—opposes my "new man." This part of me opposes God's Law. It leads me to "works of the flesh": "immorality, impurity, party spirit, envy, drunkenness, carousing, and the like." (Galatians 5:19-21)

(Note, from this list, that "flesh" does not mean "body"— i.e., sexual sins only. It includes sins of the "mind" and interpersonal sins as well as sexual sins. Nor does the "new man" refer to "mind" or "spirit" as opposed to bodily sensations. The "fruit of the Spirit is love, joy, peace, patience, kindness, goodness, faithfulness, gentleness, self-control." There are some real feelings and "body" components included in that list! We mention this to dispel the popular misidentification of "flesh" with "body" or "sex" or "emotions"— with the consequent value judgment that feelings or body functions are "bad." On the contrary, Christianity emphasizes a resurrection of the *body*—and an affirmation of a rich and positive emotional life.)

We might diagram the "two parts" of Christian parent and child, and what happens in Method I, as follows:

Parent   Child

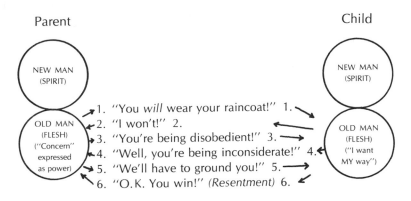

1. "You *will* wear your raincoat!" 1.
2. "I won't!" 2.
3. "You're being disobedient!" 3.
4. "Well, you're being inconsiderate!" 4.
5. "We'll have to ground you!" 5.
6. "O.K. You win!" *(Resentment)* 6.

Method I basically comes from the "old man," the desire to "lord it over" my child no matter what. As such, it addresses the "old man" in my child. Result: escalating judgmentalism, self-righteousness in me ("I'm OK—you're not"); resentment in my child. My "old man" wins—but at what a price!

Likely long-term consequences: My "old man" is strengthened to use power again the next time. His "old man" is strengthened in feelings of resentment. The "new man" in each of us may be weakened, for neither of us used the power available to us by God's Spirit.

What happens in Method II?

Parent   Child

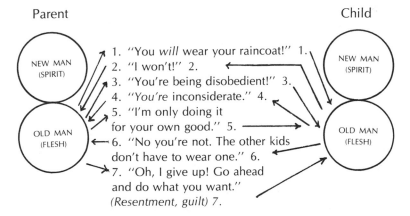

1. "You *will* wear your raincoat!" 1.
2. "I won't!" 2.
3. "You're being disobedient!" 3.
4. *"You're* inconsiderate." 4.
5. "I'm only doing it for your own good." 5.
6. "No you're not. The other kids don't have to wear one." 6.
7. "Oh, I give up! Go ahead and do what you want." *(Resentment, guilt)* 7.

61

Method II also comes from the "old man," my desire to "win." As such, it addresses the "old man" in my child, *his* desire to win. The only difference is in the outcome: His "old man" wins and I'm the one who feels resentful. In addition, my own anger and need, instead of being projected on my child, may be turned in on myself and become transmuted into guilt ("what a rotten, inadequate parent I am"), "poor me," or "I guess I am inconsiderate."

How about Method III?

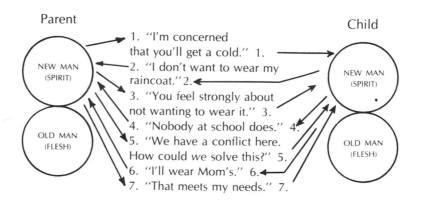

Parent   Child

NEW MAN (SPIRIT)

OLD MAN (FLESH)

1. "I'm concerned that you'll get a cold." 1.
2. "I don't want to wear my raincoat." 2.
3. "You feel strongly about not wanting to wear it." 3.
4. "Nobody at school does." 4.
5. "We have a conflict here. How could *we* solve this?" 5.
6. "I'll wear Mom's." 6.
7. "That meets my needs." 7.

NEW MAN (SPIRIT)

OLD MAN (FLESH)

Method III, beginning with an "I message," presents my need without a power demand. As such, it's my "new man" speaking to my child's "new man." Her "new man" is freed to respond to satisfy my need—willingly, out of love, rather than out of coercion. But she has a need, too, and expresses it. As I *active-listen* to her need (again, a "new man" response: "Love is patient . . .; does not insist on its own way"), her real need emerges, and both of us *together* are enabled to seek and find a solution. "I versus you" has become "we—together in Christ," who empowers us to relate to each other in love. Trusting that God's Spirit is at work in the other, we find that He is!

The Six Steps of Method III

Chapter 13 of *Parent Effectiveness Training* is invaluable in practical suggestions for putting the no-lose method to work. If you have the book, we suggest that you read that chapter carefully, noting how to apply each of the six steps of Method III:

Step 1: Identify and define the conflict. (The apparent conflict may not be the real one. "I messages" and active listening are important in surfacing what the real conflict is.)

Step 2: Generate possible alternative solutions. (Brainstorm as many as possible—and don't evaluate them at this stage in the process.)

Step 3: Evaluate the alternative solutions. (What meets *both* our needs is the criterion!)

Step 4: Decide on the best acceptable solution. (All of us commit ourselves to this solution that meets our needs. Make clear what the solution is.)

Step 5: Implement the decision. (Who is to do what, when?)

Step 6: Evaluate. (How is it working out? Modify if necessary.)

Method III in Conflicts Between Children

Method III, coupled with active listening and "I messages," can do much to resolve conflicts *between* children as well as between parent and child. Typically, when children fight, they appeal to the intervening parent with: "He started it!" "No, *he* started it!"

The parent can easily take on the role of referee and judge— only to discover that all the wisdom of Solomon can't discover who really did "start" it. And the parent's solution of the conflict quite often leads to resentment on the part of one— or even both—children. ("You always take his side." "It's not fair.")

Instead of serving as referee and judge, a parent can use the skills to facilitate the children solving their own problem in the spirit of Christ. Sometimes active listening and "I messages" alone may do the job!

You come into the back yard and discover Johnny and Kevin (a new neighbor boy) scuffling. When they see you, they break apart and glare at each other. Johnny tells you, "Kevin started pushing me." Kevin says, "No, I didn't. Besides, he took my truck."

Where's the problem in this situation? Basically, the *children* own the problem—not I, Johnny's parent. By modeling active listening and "I messages" perhaps I can help them learn these skills and resolve their conflict through really hearing each other's needs:

Parent: You're feeling very angry with each other.

Kevin: I sure am. I hate him!

Johnny: You think you're so smart. You're always pushing people around.

Kevin: Oh, yeah . . .?

Parent: Johnny, can you tell Kevin how you feel?

Johnny: Whaddya mean?

Parent: How do you *feel* right now?

Johnny: I'm really mad.

Parent: About . . .

Johnny: About his being a big bully.

Parent: Can you tell Kevin how you feel—and *describe* what he did?

Johnny: I really get mad at you, Kevin, when you push me like you just did. And . . .

Parent: Kevin, can you tell Johnny how you feel about what he just said?

Kevin: He's such a crybaby.

Parent: How do you *feel* right now?

Kevin: I'm pretty angry.

Parent: Can you tell Johnny?

Kevin: I'm feeling pretty angry with you, Johnny. I just wanted to have some fun with you and then you . . ."

Parent: You wanted Johnny to notice you?

Kevin: Yeah. I thought we could have some fun playing with my truck.

Parent: You'd like to be Johnny's friend.

Kevin: Wel-l-l, yeah!

Johnny: (thinks awhile) I'd like to be friends too, Kevin. But I don't like it when you push me. So that's why I grabbed your truck.

Parent: You like Kevin. But you don't like it when he pushes you.

Johnny: No, I don't.

Parent: (looks from Johnny to Kevin)

Johnny and Kevin: (smile embarrassedly at each other)

Kevin: Hey, do you suppose we could have some lemonade?

In this situation the parent didn't take sides. Nor did he attempt to find out who was "right" and who was "wrong." He simply recognized that the conflict was the children's problem. And he helped by active listening — i.e., he reflected their feelings — thereby indicating his acceptance of them. *And* he helped the children phrase their communications in "I messages" rather than in judgmental, "blaming you" statements. When these two skills are in operation, powered by Christian love, hostile feelings are likely to subside and a constructive resolution of the conflict is more likely to occur. When active listening and "I messages" do not resolve the conflict, they set the stage for the six steps of Method III.

Photo by Beth Slatery

CHAPTER 4

A Question of Values

When my child "owns the problem," has a need, *active listening* is a way I can relate to him in Christian love.

When I own the problem, have a need, "I messages" are a way I can share my need in Christian love, confronting rather than condemning my child or spouse.

When both of us own the problem, we can, together in Christ, attempt to resolve the conflict through Method III.

Yet there are situations in which none of these three skills is sufficient to resolve a conflict. Instead of a conflict of needs, there is a collision of values:

✔ Parent wants child to change his style of dress or length of hair. Child refuses: "It's *my* hair."

✔ Parent doesn't like child's friends. Child won't give them up. "They're my friends. I don't choose *your* friends."

✔ Child refuses to go to Sunday school or church.

✔ Child insists on listening to music or records his parents can't stand.

✔ Child won't follow in father's footsteps by studying for ministry or medical profession or . . .

✔ Child insists on going along with the gang in smoking cigarettes, drinking beer, engaging in premarital sex. Claims: "It's *my* life."

✔ Child decides to give up religion of his parents and join another denomination or become an agnostic.

Identifying a Values Collision

How can collisions of values be distinguished from conflicts of needs? In the latter, I have—or my child has—a

67

concrete and tangible need which is being frustrated by the other's behavior. Here are some examples:

✓ Son's table manners destroy my appetite.

✓ Son's driving habits cause me financial expense in car repairs and traffic tickets.

✓ Daughter's leaving a mess in the living room interferes with my entertaining my guests.

✓ Daughter's dawdling in the morning makes me late for work and imperils my job.

In all of these cases my child's behavior clearly and tangibly interferes with my needs. If "I messages" do not serve to change the behavior, problem solving (Method III) can serve to surface my child's needs that may be in conflict with my own and together we can reach a solution agreeable to both of us.

In a values collision, on the other hand, I have difficulty in coming up with a tangible need that my child's behavior is interfering with. "It's not hurting you . . ." is a typical child response — "how I wear my hair"; "who I choose for friends"; "whether I go to Sunday school or not."

In fact, the nub of my child's resistance to my influence-attempts in a values collision is just this — that he claims the freedom to "do his own thing," be his own person.

How about that claim?

Who Owns My Child?

Assuming that the readers of this book are Christian parents, i.e., parents whose values are formed by the Biblical view of what a person is and can be in Christ, we would have to say that our child is right — and wrong — in making this claim. Seeing clearly in what way he's right and wrong is terribly important — in fact, crucial — in determining what we ought to and can do in values collision.

First of all, then, let's acknowledge that there is a sense in which we need not only not to resist, but actually to affirm, our child in his drive to be "his own" person. "*My* child" is not mine in the sense of ownership. My child does not "*belong*" to me. He belongs to God—even as I belong to God. "You"—and your children—"are not your own; you were bought with a price," writes Paul (I Cor. 6:19). The same God who created me and my child as individual persons has redeemed us—"bought us back" from the power of sin and Satan—to be His.

"We are *members* one of another" (Ephesians 4:25). Like hand and foot in a human body, we are *related* to one another, but yet are different and *separate* "organs" or members in the "body" of Christ. Therefore, when I try to make my child into a carbon copy of myself, I frustrate God's unique plan and place for him in the body of Christ.

Painful as it is, I need to recognize that I cannot even force on my child the faith in Christ which makes him a member of Christ. In the last analysis, each person stands alone before God. Each person's ultimate value—his faith in Christ (or lack of it)—must be *his* faith. I cannot believe *for* my child— or force him to believe. The most I can do (and by God's grace it's a *big* most) is to model my faith and teach him the Word of God through which faith comes.

In *The Screwtape Letters,* C. S. Lewis speaks to the point of "ownership." Writing to his "junior tempter," Screwtape (a devil) says:

> The sense of ownership in general is always to be encouraged. The humans are always putting up claims to ownership which sound equally funny in Heaven and in Hell and we must keep them doing so. Much of the modern resistance to chastity comes from men's belief that they "own" their bodies —those vast and perilous estates, pulsating with the energy that made the worlds, in which they find themselves without their consent and from which they are ejected at the pleasure

of another! It is as if a royal child whom his father has placed, for love's sake, in titular command of some great province, under the real rule of wise counsellors, should come to fancy he really owns the cities, the forests, and the corn, in the same way as he owns the bricks on the nursery floor.

We produce this sense of ownership not only by pride but by confusion. We teach them not to notice the different senses of the possessive pronoun — the finely graded differences that run from "my boots" through "my dog," "my servant," "my wife," "my father," "my master," and "my country," to "my God." They can be taught to reduce all these senses to that of "my boots," the "my" of ownership. Even in the nursery a child can be taught to mean by "my Teddy-bear" *not* the old imagined recipient of affection to whom it stands in a special relation (for that is what the Enemy [God] will teach them to mean if we are not careful) but "the bear I can pull to pieces if I like." And at the other end of the scale, we have taught men to say "my God" in a sense not really very different from "my boots," meaning "the God on whom I have claim for my distinguished services and whom I exploit from the pulpit — the God I have done a corner in."

And all the time the joke is that the word "mine" in its fully possessive sense cannot be uttered by a human being about anything. In the long run either Our Father or the Enemy will say "Mine" of each thing that exists, and specially of each man. They will find out in the end, never fear, to whom their time, their souls, and their bodies really belong — certainly not to *them*, whatever happens. At present the Enemy says 'Mine' of everything on the pedantic, legalistic ground that He made it: Our Father hopes in the end to say "mine" of all things on the more realistic and dynamic ground of conquest.*

*Reprinted with permission of Macmillan Publishing Co., Inc. and Collins Publishers, from *Screwtape Letters* © C. S. Lewis 1942.

Another pertinent quote:
Christianity thinks of human individuals not as mere members of a group or items in a list, but as organs in a body — different from one another and each contributing what no other could. When you find yourself wanting to turn your children, or pupils, or even your neighbors, into people exactly like yourself, remember that God probably never meant them to be that. You and they are different organs, intended to do different things. On the other hand, when you are tempted not to bother about someone else's troubles because they are "no business of yours," remember that though he is different from you he is part of the same organism as you. If you forget that he belongs to the same organism as yourself, you will become an Individualist. If you forget that he is a different organ from you, if you want to suppress differences and make people all alike, you will become a Totalitarian. But a Christian must not be either a Totalitarian or an Individualist."*

Thank God We're Different!

Acknowledging God's ownership of our children, then, suggests that we value and affirm their uniqueness, the possibility that some of their values *may* legitimately be different from ours. Take a look again at those values collisions we listed earlier. These, at least, would seem to fall in the area of Christian freedom:

- ✔ Child's choice of hair or dress style.
- ✔ Child's choice of music.
- ✔ Child's choice of life vocation.

*Reprinted with permission of MacMillan Publishing Co., Inc. and Collins Publishers, from *Mere Christianity* © 1943, 1945, 1952 by MacMillan Publishing Co., Inc.

Their choice may not be *our* choice. But their choice does not contradict any clear Word of God. Nor does it tangibly interfere with any of our needs. Recognizing their individuality in Christ, we can respect their values choices in these and other areas in which they seek to give expression to their own developing Christian personalities.

It's really a *relief* not to have to demand conformity where God's Word allows variety. It's a *relief* to give up my efforts at playing God by claiming that *my* value-judgments are divine "musts."

I like the color blue. You think that red is the prettiest color. So—let's thank God for the whole rainbow and celebrate our diversity in Him. Let's not let purely *human* value judgments destroy our fellowship in Christ.

"One believes he may eat anything, while the weak man eats only vegetables" (Romans 14:2). That was the situation among the early Christians at Rome. Some still adhered to the custom of "kosher" meat only; some ate no meat at all; still others observed no food restrictions. The stage was set for a real values collision.

Which group was "right"?

"Let not him who eats despise him who abstains, and let not him who abstains pass judgment on him who eats; for God has welcomed him. Who are you to pass judgment on the servant of another? It is before his own master that he stands or falls" (Romans 14:3-4). Writing by inspiration of God, Paul affirms *all* the groups and strongly suggests that we be very sure that our value judgment is indeed identical with God's before we try to lay it on another person—even our child.

A better alternative is to recognize and affirm that God can be truly honored through value choices that are very different from my own: "One man esteems one day as better than another [for worship and prayer], while another man esteems

72

all days alike. Let every one be fully convinced in his own mind: He who observes the day, observes it in honor of the Lord. He also who eats, eats in honor of the Lord, since he gives thanks to God; while he who abstains, abstains in honor of the Lord and gives thanks to God." (Romans 14:5-6)

In short, many values collisions can be solved before they start, as we evaluate them on the basis of the Word of God. Are we attempting to bind our child's conscience with a value that is, after all, only a matter of our subjective preference? A matter of mere custom or fashion? Is this, really, what we want to do?

Some years ago, when many parents were hassling their children about long hair and "hippie" clothes, I saw a thought-provoking cartoon in a church magazine. Two modern-day businessmen, waiting at a stoplight, notice Jesus standing beside them. One businessman says to the other: "If that fellow would cut his hair and get rid of that robe, he could probably make something of himself."

There *are* values collisions that involve no moral issue; that, in the last analysis, are really grounded in the subjective opinions of my child and me. In these values differences I may well want to ask myself: If I cannot affirm my child's value, can I at least learn to live with it?

Teach Christian Values? Yes!

There are other values collisions which involve not only a clear Word of God, but which touch my own deepest desires for my child —

✔ that he may experience life with God through faith in Christ;

✔ that he may value the fellowship of Christians and worship of God in church attendance;

✔ that he may evidence the "fruit of the Spirit" rather than the "works of the flesh." (For example, "premarital sex"

73

in our foregoing list is a euphemism for "fornication" — a serious sin destructive of a person's relationship with God in Christ.)

Am I not called — as a Christian parent — to teach these values as God's values?

Definitely yes! Scriptural support for this position is abundant: "Train up a child in the way he should go, and when he is old he will not depart from it" (Proverbs 22:6). "These words which I command you this day shall be upon your heart; and you shall teach them diligently to your children, and shall talk of them when you sit in your house, and when you walk by the way, and when you lie down, and when you rise." (Deuteronomy 6:6ff.)

The Scriptures Show Us How

Not only do the Scriptures thus require of parents that they teach their children the content of God's Law, but they spell out *how* such instruction can be meaningful and powerful. Note that the Scriptural emphasis is on seeing ourselves — we and our children — as members of God's family because of his unmerited love (His grace) for us. God (and His Law) have a claim on us because of His steadfast love. "We love Him *because* He first loved us" (1 John 4:19). We live in "His way" out of thanksgiving for His love!

Note that emphasis in the Word to Old Testament parents: "When your son asks you in time to come, 'What is the meaning of the testimonies and the statutes and the ordinances which the Lord our God has commanded you?' then you shall say to your son, 'We were Pharaoh's slaves in Egypt; and the Lord brought us out of Egypt with a mighty hand; and the Lord showed signs and wonders, great and grievous, against Egypt and against Pharaoh and all his household, before our eyes. . . . And the Lord commanded us to do all these statutes, to fear the Lord our God, for our good always, that He might preserve us alive, as at this day. . . .' " (Deuteronomy 6:20ff.)

God's "rules" for a happy life, the moral Law or Ten Commandments, become internalized and accepted when we see Him, the Lawgiver, acting in love for us—not only in Old Testament history, but in His mighty deeds in His Son: the incarnation, the life of Christ, the cross, the empty tomb. "In many and various ways God spoke of old to our fathers by the prophets; but in these last days He has spoken to us by a Son" (Hebrews 1:1). And so we share the "good news" about Christ, talking of Him "when we sit in our house, and when we walk by the way, and when we lie down, and when we rise." We talk about Him as we know Him from the Gospels. We catch the emphasis of all the New Testament epistles: first, the marveling over God's unmerited love for us; and then, what this means for our daily living. It means Gospel power for keeping the Law, a Law which is no longer a matter of rules to *earn* God's favor, but a blueprint for the joyous life in Christ.

Teaching—formal teaching, to be sure! Through structured times like daily family devotions, evening prayer, regular attendance with the larger family of God in worship services and church schools; but especially also through informal sharing of "what Jesus means to me" in those teachable moments: the time when a young child asks, "What is the meaning of these (family and church holiday) observances?" "What happened to grandma when she died?" "Daddy, was that true what you told the policeman?"

Modeling Christian Values

We teach Christian values by teaching, in words, the facts about God and man. But more important, we teach Christian values as we *cherish* and *act* upon them in our relationships with our children. For Christian values are more than facts or information. They are what we most deeply believe in, choose, prize, and act upon. And we transmit them not simply by teaching *words* (e.g., "Forgive as you have been forgiven") but by living them out in our everyday relationships. It is as we forgive our children that they learn to be forgiving. Through our trusting them they learn to be trustworthy.

The Bible, in short, supports the importance of what psychologists call "modeling"—living your values. For it knows that children will, *on the whole*, come to value what their parents value.* Thus the first question we need to ask ourselves

---

*As this book was being written, the following song was popular. Catch what it has to say about *modeling:*

Cat's in the Cradle, by Harry Chapin

1. My child arrived just the other day;
   He came to the world in the usual way.
   But there were planes to catch and bills to pay;
   He learned to walk while I was away.
   And he was talkin' 'fore I knew it,
   And as he grew he'd say,
   "I'm gonna be like you, Dad,
   You know I'm gonna be like you."

Refrain:
   And the cat's in the cradle and the silver spoon,
   Little boy blue and the man in the moon.
   "When you comin' home, Dad?"
   "I don't know when,
   But we'll get together then;
   You know we'll have a good time then."

2. My son turned ten just the other day;
   He said, "Thanks for the ball, Dad, come on let's play.
   Can you teach me to throw?" I said, "Not today,
   I got a lot to do." He said, "That's okay."
   And he, he walked away,
   But his smile never dimmed, it said,
   "I'm gonna be like him, yeah,
   You know I'm gonna be like him." *(refrain)*

3. Well, he came from college just the other day;
   So much like a man I just had to say,
   "Son, I'm proud of you, can you sit for awhile?"
   He shook his head and he said with a smile,
   "What I'd really like, Dad,
   Is to borrow the car keys;

in a values collision is: Am I myself really living the value I want my child to accept? "But if you call yourself a Jew [Christian] and rely upon the Law and boast of your relation to God and know His will and approve what is excellent, because you are instructed in the Law, and if you are sure that you are a guide to the blind, a light to those who are in darkness, a corrector of the foolish, *a teacher of children*, having in the Law the embodiment of knowledge and truth — you then who teach others, will you not teach yourself? While you preach against stealing, do you steal? You who say that one must not commit adultery, do you commit adultery? . . . You who boast in the Law, do you dishonor God by breaking the Law?" (Romans 2:17-23)

> *Parent:* Johnny, I'm surprised at you! Don't you know that shoplifting is *stealing?*
> *Johnny:* Well, all the kids are doing it.
> *Parent:* I don't care what all the kids are doing. We're a Christian family and . . .

See you later, can I have them please?" *(refrain)*

4. I've long since retired, my son's moved away;
I called him up just the other day.
I said, "I'd like to see you if you don't mind."
He said, "I'd love to, Dad, if I can find the time.
You see, my new job's a hassle and the kids have the flu,
But it's sure nice talkin' to you, Dad,
It's been sure nice talkin' to you."
And as I hung up the phone, it occurred to me,
He'd grown up just like me;
My boy was just like me.

And the cat's in the cradle and the silver spoon,
Little Boy Blue and the man in the moon.
"When you comin' home, Son?"
"I don't know when, but we'll get together then, Dad,
We're gonna have a good time then."

Words and music by Harry Chapin and Sandy Chapin. © 1974 Story Songs, Ltd. Used by permission.

Johnny: How about that time *you* didn't pay the toll when we were going to Aunt Elinor's house?

Parent: Yeah. . . . I guess you're right. *(thinks)* Wow! I really do feel bad about that now. I haven't been honest myself—and now I'm demanding that you be honest. I really feel guilty. I'm sorry, Johnny—sorry that I gave you such a bad example. Looks like I need to do some self-examining and to talk to God about this. Will you forgive me?

Johnny: (embarrassed) Yeah. What I did is wrong too. I knew it when I did it. I don't know what got into me.

Parent: You're sorry now . . .

Johnny: Is it O.K. to ask God to forgive me?

Parent: Yes. Think we could pray together about it?

Johnny: I'd like that. Then maybe we could talk about how to give it back—the watch I took and that toll you didn't pay.

Forgiveness—possible because of the good news that God forgives me in Jesus Christ. I forgive because I am forgiven. Forgiveness: the reality that gives me the courage to see how far short I still am of being the person God intends me to be. Forgiveness: the power that frees me to confess my sin—to God and to my wife, husband, children. "Confess your sins to one another, and pray for one another, that you may be healed." (James 5:16)

Where the Power Is

We model the life in Christ to our children, recognizing and confessing that we have not yet attained it in all its fullness. Even as Christ, in human form, reflects perfectly "the glory of God and bears the very stamp of His nature" (Hebrews 1:3), so we are called to reflect "the light of the knowledge of the glory of God in the face of Christ. But we have this treasure [the good news about forgiveness in Christ] in earthen vessels, to show that the transcendent power belongs to God and not to us." (2 Corinthians 4:6-7)

Like Paul, we appeal in values collision not to our power, but to the power of God's love in Christ. "So we are ambassadors for Christ, God making His appeal through us. We beseech you on behalf of Christ, be reconciled to God. For our sake He made Him to be sin who knew no sin, so that in Him we might become the righteousness of God." (2 Corinthians 5:20)

Parent: Pam, what really concerns me about your "sleeping with" Johnny is what this is doing to your relationship with Christ.

Pam: But, Dad, I love him—and I really don't think it's any of your business. It's not hurting you—and it won't. I always take the pill.

Parent: You love Johnny—and you feel that's the important thing. I guess I can understand how you feel—but I sure can't accept it. I really feel awful about this. I feel that I've failed as a Christian parent.

Pam: So don't try that "poor Dad!" on me. It's my decision —mine and Johnny's.

Parent: O.K. You feel that I'm trying to make a decision for you. Maybe I am—but I don't want to. To be honest with you, I'd like to see you make that decision for yourself. And I suppose I've got other feelings too, like, "What would our friends think—of you and of us?" I really feel *ashamed*—for you and for us, your parents. But down underneath it all, my real and basic concern is about what's happening to your faith. I just don't see how you can be a Christian—and still persist in what you yourself know is wrong.

Pam: I don't feel it's wrong. Just sleeping with any boy— yeah, that would be wrong. But Johnny and I really care for each other. Isn't that what makes sex good—and even beautiful? How about all the married people who don't care about each other—what's so good and holy about that? How about you and Mom—you don't have a perfect marriage! That's your business, and this is mine.

Parent: Wow! You really do feel strongly about this. And so do I. Let me try to sort out where we're at. I'm relieved to hear what you feel about "just sleeping with any boy." That sure fits with the kind of person I know you are. And you love Johnny—that's the important thing for you. I can sure affirm that value too. So what it boils down to is that you feel it's O.K. to have premarital sex if you're in love. And I can't buy that value at all.

Pam: Yeah.

Parent: So how can we resolve this? Would you be willing to do some Bible searching with me—to see just what God's Word has to say about it?

Pam: I don't know. I guess that would be O.K.—as long as you don't preach at me.

Parent: I don't want to preach. And you can stop me if I do. What we'd do is look up the verses that talk about sexual relations—and marriage—and let them speak to both of us. We could use your confirmation Bible—the one with the concordance. I'd sure feel good if you'd be willing to do that.

Pam: O.K. Let's try.

In the foregoing situation, Dad nonjudgmentally shares ("I messages") his feelings of inadequacy, shame, and concern. Active listening helps simmer down his feelings and Pam's, enables Dad to hear some values he can affirm; and helps to identify the nub of the values collision. Most important, Dad has set the stage for Pam to hear the "admonition of the Gospel" rather than the commands of the Law, as together they probe the meaning of such texts as 1 Corinthians 6:13—7:9.

In this situation Dad has acted as a consultant, the second

way in which parents may influence their children's values. (Modeling — through verbal teaching of the Bible and through relating to our children in the spirit of Christ — is the fir_ way.) As consultant, he appeals not to his own authority, but to the authority of the Word of God.

Prayer Changes Things — and People

What if Pam rejects that authority? What if a child persistently clings to a value which clearly, *on Scriptural grounds*, severs his relationship with Christ? Your modeling, your attempts at being an effective consultant, have failed. And you feel terrible. What more *can* you do? You *could* attempt to force compliance, but this alternative isn't really feasible. It would literally be impossible to be with a shoplifting son or a daughter intent on sexual promiscuity *every minute of the day*. Nor would such policing of behavior — even if successful — change the *values* of the child. More likely, such a desperate attempt would intensify the child's adherence to his value.

In *Parent Effectiveness Training* Thomas Gordon suggests that the only remaining option is to accept what cannot be changed; that parents pray:

> Lord, grant me the courage to change what I can change;
> The serenity to accept what I cannot change;
> And the wisdom to know the difference.

True enough, "serenity" of a sort can be attained as we realize that each person — including our child — is finally responsible for his own actions and values — not to me, but to God. If, like Paul in his farewell address to the elders at Ephesus, we can say, "I did not shrink from disclosing to you the whole counsel of God," we can also say, "Therefore I am innocent of the blood of all of you." (Acts 20)

Yet which Christian parent, knowing that his child has actually rejected Christ, could speak these words without still feeling great anguish of heart? David literally wept when he heard about the death of his unrepentant son: "O my son Absalom, my son, my son Absalom! Would I had died instead of you, O Absalom, my son, my son!"

Christ wept over Jerusalem.

Paul experienced "great sorrow and unceasing anguish in my heart. For I could wish that I myself were accursed and cut off from Christ for the sake of my brethren." (Romans 9:2)

When all else fails, in a values collision destructive of our child's faith and life with God, we can continue to maintain the relationship with our child — all the while *praying* that God will accomplish by His Spirit what we cannot do.

Christ prayed on the cross: "Father forgive them; for they know not what they do." And some months later, through the preaching of Peter, some 3,000 "were cut to the heart," were baptized, and added to the church.

"My heart's desire and *prayer to God*" for unrepentant brethren "is that they may be saved," declared Paul (Romans 10:1), fully realizing how God had acted in his own life on that road to Damascus, changing the chief persecutor of the church into Paul, the apostle.

Three hundred years later a Christian mother prayed, year in and year out, for the conversion of her son — a son who had rejected his childhood training in the faith and was living an immoral life. The son, as he later wrote, had been "praying himself: "Give me chastity, but not yet!"

One day, his soul torn by the conflict going on within him, he cried, "How long! Tomorrow and tomorrow!" And heard the voice of a child, singing in the nextdoor garden: "Tolle lege, tollo lege" ("Take and read, take and read").

Applying these words to himself as a sign from heaven, he returned to his house, opened up a volume of St. Paul's epistles, and read the first words that met his eyes: "Not in reveling and drunkenness, not in debauchery and licentiousness, not in quarreling and jealousy. But put on the Lord Jesus Christ, and make no provision for the flesh, to gratify its desires." (Romans 13:13-14)

These words stabbed deep into his heart—and his conversion to Christianity soon followed. He is known today as *Saint* Augustine, one of the greatest of the church fathers and one of the outstanding figures of all ages.

Not surprisingly, he is known as a champion and expounder of the doctrine of the grace of God.

When all else failed—her teaching of the faith, her Christian example, her direct admonition—Monica, the mother of Augustine, still maintained the relationship with her son. Without hassling or nagging him, in prayer she pleaded with God to turn the heart of her son to Himself.

And she waited for God to act.

Photo by Mimi Forsyth

CHAPTER 5

Growing Together—in Christ

Love . . . .

Faith . . . .

Two big words in our Christian life. The "biggest" words of all. For together they describe the relationship—the most important relationship of all—the relationship between God and me. Most important because without it I literally die. St. Augustine said it truly: "Lord, You have made us for Yourself, and our hearts are restless until they find their rest in You."

Love is where it all begins. "God so *loved* the world [that includes ME!] that He gave His only Son. . . ." (John 3:16)

"God shows His *love* for us in that, while we were yet sinners, Christ died for us." (Romans 5:8)

His love in Christ reestablishes the broken relationship. "Through our Lord Jesus Christ . . . we have now received our reconciliation." (Romans 5:11)

And that, of course, is where faith enters in. For through faith we lay hold of God's love and forgiveness. In faith, worked by God's Spirit, we place our hand into the loving hands of our rescuing Father. "God so loved the world that He gave His only Son, *that whoever believes* in Him should not perish but have eternal life." (John 3:16)

"Accepted in the Beloved"

"By this doctrine of *justification* [that God forgives us freely, by His grace in Christ, through faith]," writes Luther, "the church stands or falls." It is the chief—the fundamental doctrine — of Christianity. "In my heart there reigns, and shall ever reign, this one article, namely, that faith in my dear Lord Jesus Christ, which is the sole beginning, middle, and end of all spiritual and godly thoughts which I might have at any one time, day or night."

Luther's words echo the confession of Paul: ". . . not having a righteousness of my own, based on Law, but that which is through faith in Christ, the righteousness from God that depends on faith; that I may know Him. . . ." (Philippians 3:9-10)

Being a Christian *means* that I stake my life, define my being, in terms of God's love and forgiveness for *me*. I am loved — I am "accepted in the beloved." (Ephesians 1:6)

The simple corollary of this is that I no longer need to find recognition or define my identity in terms of my success at my job, my popularity with people — *or my "success" as a parent*. I basically feel O.K. about myself — because *God* counts me as O.K. In fact, as Luther stresses in his *The Bondage of the Will*, the demand to believe myself pleasing to God is, though humanly impossible, an absolute demand of God Himself. For if *God* forgives me, counts me as His son in Christ, is it not sheer impudence on my part not to accept His love?

The consequences of *living* in the forgiveness of my sin are radical. As I review, at end of day, the events of that day, I recall those incidents in which I was impatient with my wife, foolishly boastful with my friend. I wasted a lot of time. I didn't really listen to my son.

"I really blew it, Lord!" I feel guilty. The devil — *and God's Law* — whispers, "You are indeed a sinner. Therefore you are condemned, no good, worthless, damned."

Yet God speaks another Word: "You are indeed a sinner. Therefore you are *saved*, for My Son died for sinners such as you. 'Son, be of good cheer, your sins are forgiven you.' "

I may not always feel it, but I trust "that divine logic which teaches that Christ is other than Moses [the Law] — indeed, that He is other and greater than our own conscience. . . . For if we must believe Moses and our conscience, which vexes us and convicts us by means of the Law, how much more must we believe Christ, the Lord of all things?" (Luther) "By this we shall know that we are of the truth and reassure our hearts before Him whenever our hearts condemn us; for God is greater than our hearts, and He knows everything." (1 John 3:19-20)

Forgiven, I Forgive

Forgiven, I am empowered to forgive. Loved, I am empowered to love. And because God is at work in me, I trust that He is also at work in you, the members of my family. "Because it is not in my power to fashion the hearts of men as the potter molds the clay and fashion them at my pleasure, I can get no further than their ears; their hearts I cannot reach. And since I cannot pour faith into their hearts, I cannot, nor should I, force any one to have faith. That is God's work alone, who causes faith to live in the heart. . . ." (Luther). Not force, but the Word about Christ, is the power I rely on. That's the real "power of God for salvation to every one who has faith."

"As the sun makes the day, so also does the radiance from Christ stream into all believing hearts and is at the same time in them all. As many eyes see perfectly the rays of the sun, though there is only one sun, and as everyone has this sun perfectly, and all of them have it together, so it is also with Christ. We have Him altogether, and yet each has Him in his own heart. When He comes, He lightens, rules us all through one faith. Then falsehood disappears, and the heart rightly sees God's world and work. There is then a new world, a new people, and a new light." (Luther)

And so I don't *need* to be defensive when you, my child, confront me with an accusation:

"You're not being fair!"

Nor do I need to buy into and roadblock the problems she owns:

"Mom, I could just *strangle* Margie. She's always telling lies about me."

With the love I have from Christ, I can attempt to really hear her accusation, letting God's Law and Gospel accomplish its work in me; really hear her hurt, letting God's Law and Gospel accomplish its work in her.

She: You're not being fair!

I: I expect you to keep your room neat. And yet I leave my books all over the living room. That's doesn't seem fair to you.

She: It sure doesn't. It's really hard to dust and vacuum around all that stuff.

I: Well, I can sure appreciate that. When I'm working on an article, I always seem to refer to a lot of books—and leaving them out helps me to save time. I guess I just didn't think about the extra work it was causing you. I'm sorry.

She: Well, that's why my room is such a mess too—with homework and that hobby kit I've been working on. . . .

I: Sounds like we both need to work on this, to figure out what will satisfy all our needs best. . . .

Daughter: Mom, I could just *strangle* Margie. She's always telling lies about me.

Mom: Wow! Sounds like you're really angry with Marge.

Daughter: Am I! You know what she did? She told Dana that I didn't like her—and that's why I didn't invite her to my party.

Mom: You're upset that Marge would say something that's not true. You *do* like Dana.

Daughter: Yes, I like Dana a lot . . . except, of course, when she acts so uppity.

Mom: Sometimes you don't like her.

Daughter: No, I don't. Like last week, just before my party, she really snubbed me at recess—just cut me out when she and her friends were talking. *That's* why I didn't invite her to my party.

Mom: You were hurt by the way she acted.

Daughter: Yeah, and I guess I just wanted to get even with her. But now it's a real mess. Margie told her I don't like her—and now I've had a fight with Margie—and they all think I'm pretty awful.

Mom: It's going from bad to worse. You really want to be friends—and it's turning out that Dana and Marge and some of the others don't like you.

Daughter: They hate me—and, and I hate myself too! I really feel bad about not inviting Dana. It was a rotten thing to do.

Mom: You feel guilty about the way you treated Dana.

Daughter: Mom, I really do. She *did* snub me. But we've always been friends. And I guess I should have asked her why she was acting that way—instead of just trying to get even.

Mom: You feel now that there was a better way to handle it. You're sorry that you didn't invite her to the party.

Daughter: I'm sorry—and I don't know what to do.

Mom: You're wondering what to do.

Daughter: Tell her the way I feel—will she still be mad at me? Or try to act like nothing's happened? Or what?

Mom: (*silence*)

Daughter: I guess deep down I really know. I was pretty mean to her. And I am sorry. And I'm going to tell her and ask her to forgive me. And—I guess I'll talk to Margie too.

Mom: You feel relieved, now that you've decided what to do. But it won't be easy.

Daughter: It will be pretty hard. So I better go over to her house right now. Will you have time to talk when I get back?

Mom: There'll be some time before supper.

Daughter: Thanks, Mom.

No "religious" words were spoken in these dialogs, but yet the *spirit* of Christ was there—in attitudes which facilitated genuine repentance and a loving consideration of one another's needs. Both situations, of course, could well be reflected on, later, and related to family devotions and prayer.

Forgiven, I Confront

In both situations, active listening, powered by the parent's reliance on God's forgiveness of himself/herself and the child, facilitated spiritual growth. Similarly, it's God forgiveness in Christ which empowers me, the parent, to confront my child in a spiritually nourishing way when *I* "own the problem."

It's Sunday morning. Dad discovers that John didn't rake the front lawn yesterday, as he promised he would.

Dad: Hey, John, I'm really upset. You told me that you raked the front lawn, but it doesn't look like you did.

John: Well, I *did* do some of it. Then David came over and we started playing catch. And before I knew it, it got too dark to finish.

Dad: I was counting on you to do it yesterday while I seeded the garden. Now I feel disappointed that it isn't done —and I don't have time to work on it myself today. Remember, I have to go on my business trip after church.

John: Well, I'm sorry I let you down. Tell you what—I'll get at it right after church. I really will.

Dad: That sounds O.K. to me. But I'm still bothered that you told me you finished when you didn't.

John: Yeah, I know. I guess that was a lie. I knew you'd get mad if I told you it wasn't done—and I hoped you wouldn't notice the leaves this morning.

Dad: You felt bad about it yesterday—scared that I'd yell at you.

John: Yeah. But it was a chicken thing to lie about it.

Dad: Well, let's forget about it now, O.K.? I feel pretty good about your sharing with me how you felt. And I feel relieved that the job will be done today.

John: You can count on me. Hey, isn't it time to leave for church?

Dad's nonjudgmental confrontation flows from the confidence in his own status as a forgiven sinner. And his confidence that John—even though he has lied—still has God's Spirit. He doesn't need more judgmental blame laid on him—but rather to be helped to surface the blame that's already there in his heart, so that he and Dad can deal with it. John's confession and Dad's forgiveness reestablish, perhaps strengthen, their relationship with each other and their confidence in a forgiving God.

Notice, again, how Dad's attitude and approach fit the Biblical model of Christian admonition: "Brethren [note—I approach him as still a *brother* in Christ], if a man is *overtaken* in any trespass [the trespass doesn't define who he is; I see him as an erring *brother* rather than an *erring* brother], you who are spiritual [sounds like that's what parents are—people who are more mature in their Christian growth] should *restore* him [not "wipe him out"] *in a spirit of gentleness* [judgmental "you statements" or confronting "I statements"?]. Look to yourself, lest you too be tempted. [I approach him as a fellow-sinner. He and I together stand under God's judging Law—*and His forgiving love.* Judging myself as "holier than thou" puts *me* under that Law and its condemnation. I need to be aware that responding to his possible defensive anger with judgmental anger of my own destroys both of us.] Bear one another's burdens, and so fulfill the law of Christ." That's the new commandment Jesus gave us: "Love one another *as I have loved you.*" Wow! When I think of His forgiving love for me, what else can I do *but* love you as He does? (Galatians 6:1-2)

Forgiven, We Strengthen One Another

Again, it's when I see myself as a forgiven sinner—with you, my fellow members of the body of Christ in my family—that we are enabled to build one another up in our Christian faith and life. It's truly a "no lose"—everybody wins—situation, when I see the relevance of "Be subject *to one another*" standing at the beginning of the Biblical text which deals with family relations, Ephesians 5:21—6:4.

A Christian "no lose" approach to family conflicts of needs becomes possible when I see *myself* as both sinner *and* saint— through Christ. Accepted in Christ, I'm free to get in touch with my real feelings and to share them transparently and openly with you, the members of my family. Accepted in Christ, I'm not threatened when you honestly share your feelings and needs with me. For I see you as a person redeemed by Christ, in whom His Spirit is at work. "I versus you" has become "we—together in Christ," who empowers us to meet each other's needs, to heal each other's hurts, to relate to each other in love. New man speaks to new man. Trusting each other, we're open to the influence of the Spirit.

One Body—in Christ

When values collisions come, I recognize that even as Christ is shaping me into a unique image of Himself, so is He at work in you, shaping you into a unique image of Himself. You are not to be a carbon copy of me, but a reflection of Him whose you are. We are both parts of His body—but we are separate and unique members of that body. Therefore I will listen with respect as you share your deepest values and ask that you listen with respect to mine. Together, we can help one another to test our values in terms of Christ, affirming our diversity and celebrating our unity in Him, growing together "to mature manhood, to the stature of the fullness of Christ."

The only value that could divide us from one another is a value that divides us from Him. "Even we have believed in Christ Jesus, in order to be justified by faith in Christ, and not by works of the Law, because by works of the Law shall no one be justified" (Galatians 2:16). If what you value destroys your faith in Christ, we cannot help but seek to restore you to Him. We shall neither hassle you to "be good" nor appeal to our own "righteousness." But rather, as "ambassadors for Christ," let God make "His appeal through us," pointing you again to His marvelous love in Christ: "We beseech you on behalf of Christ, be reconciled to God. For our sake He made Him to be sin who knew no sin, so that in Him we might become the righteousness of God."

And we shall seek to model Christ in our lives with you, praying that *God* will restore you to Himself.

For, finally, we see ourselves as "members one of another" in the body of Christ. "Speaking the truth in love," we seek to "grow up in every way into Him who is the head, into Christ, from whom the whole body, joined and knit together by every joint with which it is supplied, when each part is working properly, makes bodily growth and upbuilds itself in love." (Ephesians 4)